MOUNTAIN HIGH

MOUNTAIN RESCUE

MOUNTAIN HIGH

MOUNTAIN RESCUE

Peggy Parr

ILLUSTRATIONS BY DAISY DE PUTHOD

FULCRUM • 1987

Copyright © 1987
Fulcrum Incorporated

Book Design by Frederick R. Rinehart
Front Cover Photo by Reg Francklyn
Back Cover Photo by Nuri Valbona
Book Illustrations by Daisy de Puthod

LIBRARY OF CONGRESS CATALOGING-IN-PUBLICATION DATA
Parr, Peggy
Mountain High/Mountain Rescue

Includes Index
1. Mountaineering – Colorado – Search and rescue operations
– Case studies
I. Title   II. Parr, Peggy, 1923
GV200.183.P37   1986   363.1'4   86-25773
ISBN 1-55591-005-X

FULCRUM, INC.
GOLDEN, COLORADO

*The incidents in this book took place in
Colorado between 1981 and 1986.
They are faithfully recorded here
without embellishment of any kind.*

*A portion of the proceeds
of this book are being donated
to search and rescue activities
in Colorado.*

Contents

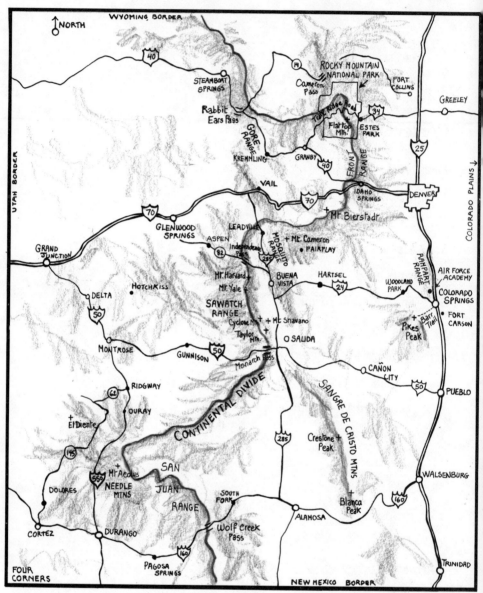

Artist Conception

Foreword

The nation's "search and rescue" community is small, no more than the population of a small town, but the volunteer service provided by these skilled teams of individuals far exceeds simple numbers. They are people who venture "beyond the roadhead," regardless of weather and terrain, to help the victims of back-country accidents. What fire departments, ambulance services and other public safety agencies do in cities and towns, search and rescue teams do in the severest environment – rock, forest, cold and blizzard.

The people who choose rescue as an avocation are remarkable. They're driven by an overabundance of adrenaline, an inexhaustible compassion for those in need and a hunger for high adventure. They must train hard, some more than 200 hours a year.

Peggy Parr has all three qualities plus the know-how, as do her colleagues on El Paso County Search and Rescue and the other teams – whether they be in Oregon, New Hampshire, Colorado or California. Driven to help, they respond at any hour, in any weather, to the call for help from a sheriff, park ranger, the state patrol or other agency. Their reward is neither salary nor recognition, but is in the joy of saving a life.

These, then, are the actual experiences of Peggy Parr. She, like others in her avocation, has felt the high of mountain rapture, the panic of going to the edge, the sorrow of being too late and the reward of preventing a death.

Since her introduction to mountain rescue in 1981, Peggy has responded to more than 100 missions. She's become a veteran, a skilled, highly motivated rescue mountaineer who has proven her value time and again. Today she's an eagerly sought resource in any mission, in any terrain and in any weather. She's become a mentor to younger women across the West and an inspiration to those who feel the years encroaching on their youth.

Peggy and her husband, Jim, have four children: Jacqui, a graduate of Yale who's a New York banker, Joey at Vassar, Terence at Purdue and Jim Jr. in his second year of law at the University of Denver.

J. Hunter Holloway
Mission Coordinator, Colorado
Vice President, Mountain Rescue Association

After completion of a mission, Skee gathers equipment while Tom talks to Peggy.

1. INTRODUCTION

The hot sun of a Colorado autumn burned through my shirt while I stood quietly in the scrub oak on the mesa watching red-tailed hawks soaring in the wind currents. I glanced across the canyon where two people stood on a thin ledge above a granite cliff high on Cutler Mountain, just west of my Colorado Springs home. Through my field glasses I watched as, suddenly, one of them slipped from the ledge and plunged to the steep slope below, bouncing, spinning, crashing against the sharp rocks. I raced along a deer trail into Cheyenne Canyon to seek help. A rescue team had just brought down a young woman from a waterfall tumble on the same mountain; as the sirens carried her away, I burst upon them with word of another accident. They listened to me in disbelief; surely it was the waterfall tragedy that I had witnessed.

While the questions flowed, I stared at the youthful team members with their orange shirts, their helmets and technical climbing gear – a pang of envy shot through me. I could never join a mountain rescue team. The decades spent climbing peaks and running rivers, tasting dangers, feeling adrenaline, had made me a seasoned mountaineer; however, the gathered years marked me down in the eyes of the young. To them I was a mossback.

When my frustration was approaching the explosion point, a rusty-bearded rescuer asked two members to accompany me to the cliff where I had seen the hiker fall. After a struggle through the steep scrub oak, we came upon the crumpled body of a young girl lying barely conscious on the sharp rocks. When the team gathered and tied her in a litter, I was asked to be a rope handler for the brake system that lowered her off the mountain. Afterwards the rusty-bearded man ignored my wrinkles and asked me to join their team, El Paso County Search and Rescue.

The two girls who fell that day, one from the waterfall and the other down the cliff, were sisters, and both would recover except for a rigid ankle, a missing kidney and countless scars to remind them of their mountain picnic. As for me – ironically, their accidents raised my life to new heights.

Why would I, no longer young, with four children out of the nest, a life of freedom, plenty of friends, want to join this rescue team? Yes, to help others, but more to swim against the mainstream, and definitely to prevent my mind from rotting. Someone who has never experienced a fading mind and weakening muscles cannot appreciate the alarm it triggers.

I admit I want to ease the pain of breaks and fractures, attempt to soothe frantic parents. I don't relish handling decomposing bodies on mountainsides, yet at those moments I've experienced depths of thought not possible in a funeral parlor. Now I look with cynicism on beauty and fame, for I've seen the effects on man of animals and insects, of cold and rain, when the heart no longer beats. I'm humbled to realize that after death a human body is no different from a dead elk lying on the alpine meadow.

In my earlier days, my studies, my profession, and my own business had been landscape architecture. The field was exciting and definitely challenging. I traveled a lot and stood with respect before European cathedrals and bridges, meandered for hours through English perennial gardens, delighted in the perfect symmetry and serenity of Japanese designs. But I also craved a rawer kind of adventure, and so I wandered up

Central American volcanoes, rafted down Mexican rivers and traveled across the African veldt. It was in these settings that I really came alive. In Africa's Great Rift Valley, for example, I flew back through the ages to my primitive origins, and later followed pigmies over rutted trails into the Ituri Forest, to sit in huts of bent saplings and banana leaves and feel their simple lives. I am born into civilization but crave the wilderness.

Early on I found the adventure needed in my life, but couldn't find the husband, Jim, until 38 years had swiftly passed. Although he wasn't interested in the woods and summits, his inner strength attracted me, and I saw his soft, brown eyes as those of a deer and his shape that of a friendly bear. We began a family, one a year, and soon left crowded Los Angeles to raise the four children in Colorado Springs.

No volunteer group ever remains static. People join our rescue team without any idea of what a member does, or they leave our rescue team due to job or military transfers, or – impossible to believe – for lack of interest. Members tend to drift in and out, like clouds before and after a rain. Some contribute much before they depart; others fade away without leaving a trace. The rusty-bearded member, Ron Holladay, a building contractor in his 40s, founded the group and was its president for 11 years, before he chose to leave because the missions ceased to challenge him. He had done it all, knew it all and felt the need of a fresh call to battle. Now he is spurred on by an interest in horses, roping and the prairie.

I asked Mel Druelinger, a 45-year-old, bearded professor with a Ph.D. in chemistry, what made him such a charger in the field during a mission. After all, he was born and raised in Indiana – how could the mountains get into his blood in that gently rolling state? After the usual answers – feeling of satisfaction, need for a challenge, maybe an adrenaline junkie, desire to help others – I detected a deeper reason. Mel teaches organic chemistry, day after day, without seeing results in a student until some years have passed. A mission begins and ends in hours, or in one to two to three days, and gives immediate satisfaction. To do the best one can, see the results, then go back to normal life, gives one a sense of accomplishment, a feeling that a job is finished, a goal completed. Only the critique remains to be done.

Mel isn't typical; he's exceptional in his commitment to rescue work. Still, other men on the team mirror his devotion. Tom Frazer, 43-years-old and our president for the past five years, is representative of our middle-aged members. An electrical engineer with Digital Equipment Corporation, with greying hair and excess pounds, he doesn't seem a courageous rescuer. But get him in the driver's seat of a vehicle with power to four wheels, and he aggressively assaults mountainsides, roaring, "Hang on!!"

On my second mission, when I was still polite to the men, I watched Tom in action. We had just brought down the frozen body of a murder victim to Gold Camp Road, when a passing car reported a truck rollover deeper in the mountains. Bringing the corpse with us, and with Tom at the wheel, we careened at frantic speed along the skinny road, hard with glare-ice. Through narrow tunnels and around nasty curves, we sped and slid while I cried, "You're going too fast!" The men, accustomed to Tom, laughed and asked me, "What's the matter?" Such road behavior isn't consistent with the team's obsession with safety on a mission. In fact, more than one victim, not to mention team member, has suffered car sickness when our rescue vehicle gobbled the curves of a mountain too swiftly.

In spite of his driving, Tom has a certain steadiness and a great perception of people to accompany his considerable rescue knowledge. His sympathetic radio reply, "I understand," heard from base during night missions when gales blow over us and ice pellets sting our faces, can keep the mist of frustration and loneliness from gathering in a weary searcher's eyes.

Other middle-aged members, dignified and quiet-spoken, amaze me with their chameleonlike changes. One afternoon human footprints found in mud along the side of Pikes Peak were reported to us after an unsuccessful search was closed down. Five of us drove up the Toll Road and discovered that a bear had lumbered through the mud and left "bear feet," as opposed to the report of "bare feet." Suddenly our pagers announced a mission elsewhere. I was astonished to see the fellows in their 30s and 40s leap into the air at 9,000 feet and gallop a half-mile to our rescue vehicle. Not into galloping, I arrived late and last.

No generic rescuer exists, for we vary too much in our ages, appearance and behavior. Rich Laubhan, a bearded electrical engineer in his early 30s and thinning of thatch, is quiet, cautious, controlled and steady as the mountain rain. Then there is Rod Willard, a fine ambulance paramedic in his late 20s, who drives as though always on an emergency call, grows a butter-yellow mop above his orange beard, and is as wild as a kestrel hawk caught in the hand. Rudy Pederson, a big, muscular fellow just out of the Marines and working three jobs, always wears a grin wide as a gaping crevasse below his shining eyes. Dick Stienmier, a physician with 50 years, greying hair and beard to match, is distinquished-looking despite his shy smile and boyish laugh, and can be found in the front of many missions. In contrast, George Rice, about the same age, rarely goes into the field (he is set a bit heavy), but can run a mission like few others. Kevin Classen, young in face and age, loves sitting before the radios in the communication trailer during a mission (a duller job I can't imagine). Whereas Skee Hipszky, his face obscured by his beard, strides assertively through the mountains with powerful legs and lungs, and quietly directs the movements of our members.

With our team a double search is always going on – the quest for people who can be molded into competent rescue members, and the pursuit of money to buy such group needs as ropes, fuel for our two vehicles, radios and climbing equipment. The money eventually comes in, usually as the result of begging letters sent out to local businessmen; or, indirectly, from a mountain safety publication in which industry places advertisements; or possibly as a donation from a civic organization. Also, now and then, funds are given by a victim, or his family, as a donation, a way of saying "thank you." Fund raising is a bore to most of us, but, luckily, there is always some member who takes pleasure in this critical job. Our personal equipment – clothing, boots, helmet, rock gear, ice axe, crampons, snowshoes, sleeping gear – is purchased out of our own pockets. A large sum for a young person, but the list can be gathered gradually.

Initially, most people interested in filling out a team application are taken in as probationaries. The training of new members, a two-and-half-day rigorous weekend every four months, follows. If they fit into the group, are comfortable with cliffs and have a controllable ego, then the board considers them for regular membership in three or four months.

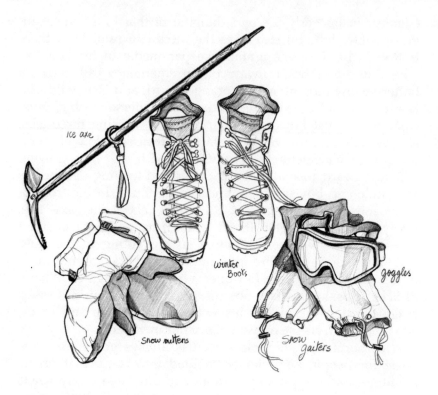

ice axe

Winter Boots

goggles

snow mittens

snow gaiters

A few note the time commitment necessary and drift away. Immaturity in 18-year-olds – the youngest we take – may cause problems, and they rarely become regular members. Some women take a look at the rock work we do and never come back; others look at the camaraderie of the team and come aboard. A few women join and are captured by our bachelors, remaining on the roster as wives. Usually, though, there are no more than two or three women on our team at a time, which is strange in this day when women are boldly demonstrating their courage and compassion. Annie Pettinari, a strong, young member with a lovely face, was hired by Colorado Springs as a city firewoman, the first and only. No other woman has been able to meet her abilities.

When women come on the team I scrutinize them carefully. They must prove themselves to me, but the men love them right away for they are new bait for teasing. On a mission, the men don't give the women a load to carry; everybody takes whatever weight they can handle – if no load is carried, nothing is said. The men on the team are kind to us, but

I become upset when a man helps a new woman probationary to cross a stream or climb up a cliff. If she can't do it on
her own, then she shouldn't join us, is my philosophy.

Once in a while probationaries draw the growls of regular
members. Sometimes new members with rock-climbing experience can put on an arrogant face and don't want to practice
the basic techniques we use on our missions. Rock rescues
can be done several ways, but we teach just one method, to
avoid confusion and increase safety.

The camaraderie and warmth and care I feel for a fellow
member increases as the number of missions with that member increases. The trials and joys of a mission bond us
together with an insoluble glue. To make your way together
down a mountain for hours in an inky night allows for depth
in a conversation that wouldn't be plumbed in town.

The team isn't always smooth and loving, for in any group
of self-motivated, Type A volunteers, disagreements, factions
and splits will surface. The personal ambitions and strong na-
tures of members are evident. Wimps don't join. Some members overload their lives, both professionally and voluntarily,
causing lack of sleep and inner stress by trying to do too much
in too little time. Still, our egos demand stroking and success.
Rescue work satisfies that craving, from the 20s to the 60s.

At best, nothing is perfect. There are hardships to remember: the nights on bivouac when I lay exhausted, turning for
hours, and praying for sleep, the ground hard against my
hips; or the panic I felt on Mount Yale when I jumped from
the helicopter into a dense cloud of powder snow churned up
by the rotor blades close overhead, fearing head-loss and
drowned lungs; then my exhaustion on Mount Cameron
from an endless litter-carry over massive rocks that swal-
lowed our legs while the crumpled aircraft threatened to fall
on us from above.

But the rich memories remain: the rasp of fiberglass sleds
against the snowcrust and our black figures in the ghostly
moonlight as we hauled an old man and three children off
the face of Pikes Peak. I recall hiking for hours down a
wooded valley alongside wild orchids and a racing stream,
the air filled with green mist in the downpour.

During these days and nights of mountain struggle I reach
my heights, I have a reason for being, I feel raw nature – and I
am filled with a sense of completeness.

Rescuers on snowshoes pull Steve in a sled over the eight-foot-deep snow.

2. CHRISTMAS MIRACLE

The mountains of Colorado in winter are inhospitable to single-engine aircraft.

"If we crash, don't run uphill – the two rotors wind down slowly and will chop off your head. And remember, we're going to bounce around in the storm up there." Chilling words barked by Captain Ron Liss, an Army coordinator, while we listened – seven volunteers from the El Paso County Search and Rescue – our bodies huddled on the red canvas benches deep in the belly of the Chinook helicopter. My mouth was dry, my palms drenched in sweat, while waiting for my first helicopter lift-off.

We sat along the fuselage wall, heavy boots jammed against a wobbly stack of backpacks, ice axes and snowshoes that wormed down the center of the aircraft. I tugged at my helmet strap and poked my earplugs deeper. Ed Trujillo, a 20-year-old team member facing me across the gear, caught my eye, and without smiling we raised our thumbs. I mumbled prayers. His black eyes mirrored the fear in mine.

Mel, an Air Force Academy professor with many missions

behind him, had warned me yesterday, "This mission's difficult. Only winter-experienced members are being taken. Can
you go, Peggy?"

"Yes, I want to go!" But he hadn't mentioned a helicopter. . .

An emergency locator transmitter was sending radio signals from somewhere west of Buena Vista, in the Collegiate
Peaks, where the stout shoulders of Mount Yale, Mount Harvard and Mount Columbia rise dramatically over 14,000 feet
to pierce awesome winter storms. By federal law all private
planes carry this electronic device – or they're supposed to –
so the Civil Air Patrol and rescue teams can find them if they
crash. The ELT, as we call it, isn't large, only quart size, yet it
has its own antennae and a battery that will broadcast for 72
hours. It fastens into the aircraft tail. A crash impact closes a
switch that triggers the signal; in spite of only 100 milliwatts
of power, it can be heard over vast distances.

Mel was silent for a moment, then in a puzzled voice added, "No plane's been reported missing – not even overdue –
but maybe the pilot didn't bother to file a flight plan. Since
these waves are from the Continental Divide, it could be a
plane crash. Anyway, we've got to search."

The Civil Air Patrol had flown the previous day trying to
pin down the exact source of the signals, which bounced off
cliffs and mountainsides, coming in horizontally and vertically from everywhere like a playful echo.

Mel said we'd tramp through the snow carrying an electronic directional finder, which picks up the incessant undulating cry and tells us its direction. These readings are radioed
down to base, the Civil Air Patrol plots them on a map, and
eventually the crash is pinpointed.

Since the Chinook helicopter from Fort Carson near
Colorado Springs, was grounded by weather that afternoon
during Christmas week of '81, we had driven in a four-wheel-
drive over 100 stormy miles to the search at Buena Vista. The
four oldest of us called ourselves the "Geriatric Squad." The
road through the bleak moonscape was coated with milky ice;
we slid cautiously over Wilkerson Pass, across South Park
and down Trout Creek Pass.

Sneaking into the fire station, our mission base, late that
evening, Mel introduced me to our field coordinator, Captain

Ron, from the Army's Fort Carson, south of Colorado Springs. He was sprawled in his longjohns across the coiled hoses on a massive fire engine. Outside, the temperature was below zero; inside, a ceiling heater blasted hot air across the station and kept the fire truck motors warm and ready to go.

I greeted Ron like an old hand, but inside I shrank with insecurity. The small bit of confidence I had gained in rescue work since joining our team a few weeks ago abruptly drained away. Here was a scared lady out of her territory. Would Captain Ron nail down my boots in base and tell me to sit and help with the radio? Was I a little old lady wearing hiking boots but too old to go into the field? I'd soon know.

The third bay of the fire station was minus a fire engine, but it was not empty. Emergency gear climbed high against the wall. The concrete floor was smothered in down sleeping bags – each containing a sleeping man – and from the center of the floor rose a plastic table and some odd chairs, looking like a modern sculpture under the glaring light. A toilet, sink and water heater were crowded in a corner, barely hidden by a head-high wall, the top open to all. I threw my bag and pad in front of the truck on the only visible concrete and crawled inside. A steel pillar and an overbearing engine tire kept me in my place. If the alarm rang I'd have to move fast or be run over.

Deeper into the frigid night a volunteer group from Boulder – Rocky Mountain Rescue – stormed into the station. They bellowed like bulls while stamping their feet to shed snow. Their manliness and vigor intimidated me. No women accompanied their team.

We arose silently in the dark at 6:00. I ate granola and powdered milk, glued with hot water from the sink, while Rocky Mountain Rescue men took out backpacking stoves and squatted to cook powdered eggs and grey oatmeal. After eating I walked outside and stood shivering in the snow beside the icy street. Across the valley stretched the gently folded foothills of the Collegiate Peaks, buried under deep layers of snow that glowed pink from the first rays of the morning sun. Lying like a scarf across the high peaks was a heavy, ashen cloud. The romantic scene tranquilized my acute anxiety.

Inside the hot station Captain Ron shouted the day's briefing: "One team climbs up the east ridge of Mount Columbia; another will be dropped off by Chinook on the summit and will hike down a south ridge while taking readings." I cringed to hear my name on the summit team – a 14,073-foot summit. The fire station, located at 8,000 feet, was now 10 degrees below zero. Maybe I'd taken on too much.

I encased my body in every garment I'd brought. Down hood and wool balaclava wrapped my head. Two woolen underwear tops covered my chest, plus a heavy wool sweater and down jacket, topped by two windbreakers, to round me out. Two pairs of woolen underwear bottoms and wool trousers, covered by wind pants, stiffened my legs. The insulated boots were two sizes too large. Down mittens, wool socks and gaiters finished me off. I was a strange sight.

Suddenly the command "Let's go!" rang out like the fire bell. Outside, a string of four-wheel-drive pickups pulsed eagerly, ranchers at the wheel, the airport our destination. The airport was humble, a large field split by a runway of unswept blacktop and punctuated by a windsock flying from a pole. A dried crop of tumbleweeds clustered around our trucks. Looking toward the mountains, I realized a shroud concealed the windswept summit of Mount Columbia. Soon I'd be jumping onto its crest hugging my snowshoes.

"Peggy, where'd you get those clumsy old snowshoes? They must be five feet long."

"At a pawn shop eight years ago. They've been a decoration on our wall at home. Never used 'em." I'd never worn snowshoes before, though my ice axe was an old friend from Rainier, Hood and Shasta.

Base radioed to the knot of rescuers waiting beside the runway: "No one, absolutely no one, goes on the mountain without an avalanche beacon." I began to tremble at this suggestion of suffocation. The beacon, size of a cigarette case, hangs from the neck against the chest for battery warmth. The airport briefing for the beacon began, "Now for you new people, when we get up there put it on "sending cycle"; then if anyone's caught in an avalanche, we'll turn to "receiving cycle" and use the earplugs. We crisscross the avalanche listening carefully; under the highest sound intensity lies the buried person." The lightweight shovel lashed to our packs was for fast digging.

As the Chinook approached, I heard a low throb from deep in its throat. Six tiny wheels snuggled against its dark insect body. It seemed alien. The brown, boxlike austerity was relieved by bright red canvas stretched across the small circular windows: blood from a beating heart. A turbine engine on each side of the tail exhaled hot breath. The two rotors were long and slender, like an insect's antennae. It seemed assembled from leftover parts.

The aircraft approached over the white foothills and hovered next to the runway to flex its muscles. The 125-mph rotor wash threw great quantities of dirt and snow into the air. Tumbleweeds danced wildly about the blades. When the roaring machine landed, I threw the backpack over my shoulder and, ice axe and snowshoes in hand, scurried under the whirling blades to board.

Though other rescuers carried heavy packs with internal frames, mine was an external frame Kelty, a relic from the Middle Ages. It was light: a headlamp, down sleeping bag, thin pad, but no tent (I hoped to be the other occupant of somebody's two-man tent). For a possible two days in the field, I carried water and a firm cake of dried fruits, nuts, chocolate, honey, flour, butter and eggs – nothing more. When my liter of water was gone, I'd find a supply at occasional warm springs or break through the snow and ice covering streams. In winter I might not recognize the rare stream or water hole that isn't suitable for drinking water – those devoid of life due to a mineral substance like arsenic or lithium present in the water. A mossy, even stagnant, pool is better. If time allows, the water can be boiled 20 minutes or purified with a tablet. Usually I just drink the water, and treat any problem later if some critter shows up inside me. Dehydration is a grave matter. The classic statement – you can survive three weeks without food; three days without water; three minutes without air – is the 11th Commandment. I should have carried a backpacking stove and fuel. I do now.

With the morning sun behind us we lifted off toward Mount Columbia. I glanced out the small window to see our shadow cross rail fences and the backs of grazing horses in the frozen fields. Something was missing in the shadow – I realized the Chinook had no wings.

As the motors strained to gain elevation in North Cottonwood Canyon, we were alert for aircraft wreckage on the cliffs crowding above and beside us. Rigid Engelmann spruce rose below our fuselage; the rotor wind exploded a wild snowstorm out of the heavily laden trees.

"Yagi"
ELT Sensor

Captain Ron had chosen four rescuers to jump out onto a sloping canyon wall to take Yagi readings. The Yagi is a five-foot long collapsible antenna used to determine the direction a radio signal is coming from. Two rows of sensory rods pick up radio waves from the ELT – the closer the Yagi to the transmitter, the louder the undulating cry. The rescuers grabbed packs and leaped out the door into chest-deep snow. A rotor-driven blizzard of frigid air and snow crystals rushed into the fuselage and settled over us. Dragging their heavy packs and wincing at the whirling front rotor two feet above, they forged a trail downhill and began to take readings hurriedly. When a powerful gust of wind tilted the hovering Chinook, the pilot threw on full power and we roared into the air, deserting the men below.

They radioed Captain Ron, "The ELT is closer to Yale than Columbia." The plan changed: we'd be dropped higher in the same narrow canyon. Goodbye, Columbia! Moments later we banked sharply, circling a white jewel in the black spruce. A crewman opened the rear ramp, lay on his stomach and mumbled landing directions to the pilots by intercom while the crew chief hung out the side door.

Suddenly Captain Ron rose and lifted his palms. Time to go! I whipped off my seat belt, grabbed my gear, and was first to stand on the ramp above an unknown depth of snowflakes. Talking to the crewman was out, thanks to the plugs in my ears and the deafening blast from the rotors. I caught his eye and pointed to the snow and myself. He nodded his head. I walked to the ramp edge and turned again to face him. Another nod of his head.

I begged, "O God, help me!" and jumped six feet through the air and submerged to my shoulders in the powder. The rotor gale was whipping the crystals into a frenzy. I gasped for breath and drew in the blizzard, which melted in my lungs. With eyes closed I kept my head low and tried to break through the bank of snow ahead. Glancing behind, I saw my companions crouched low, following like elephants in my trench. To stay beneath or beside the machine was imprudent; if it lost power, we risked a crushing or beheading. Suddenly I had a vision of my husband Jim selling our home and my flower garden after my funeral – me having been decapitated by a rotor blade. A surge of adrenaline flowed and I struggled faster. Then the gale and roar ceased, and my panic subsided. The Chinook lifted and pulled away at a sharp angle. I collapsed and panted, "Thank God."

"I've never been so glad to see a chopper leave," moaned Ed, with eyes closed, stretched on his back over the snow.

I glanced at a stranger among us, Chuck Demerest – the team leader and a member of Rocky Mountain Rescue. He was a startling sight against the severe black and white surrounding us. His flowing and unclipped beard was straw yellow, golden yellow and orange. Under a wool cap I saw a fringe of yellow curls, freckles and bright-blue eyes.

When snowshoes were strapped on our boots, Chuck ordered, "Peggy, come with me; and you three break a trail down the canyon. If the Chinook can't pick us up tonight, we'll need a route out."

Rich, a fellow El Paso member, spoke quietly to me, "You may need this." He handed me a radio, which I tucked under my clothing next to the avalanche beacon.

Chuck and I started up Mount Yale into a brooding winter storm. My canteen runneth over in this late morning. Perhaps Chuck chose me because I had led out from the Chinook. How ironic! He didn't know how frightened I was. But once the helicopter left I felt intoxicated with joy in the silent fairyland of snow and spruce and aspen.

We crossed the clearing and entered a miniature aspen forest. Chuck broke trail briskly beside a meandering ice- and snow-covered stream. The fresh snowflakes compressed silently under our snowshoes; the only sound was our heavy breathing.

I shattered the silence with, "I'll break trail when you get tired."

"No," he quickly answered, "I'll break trail. We're on a rough mission and I want to be sure you can walk out."

"No, I'll lead half the way, you lead half the way. We'll trade. That's the way we'll do it." No more was said; nothing like a little "macha" from a lady.

While Chuck took Yagi readings, I struggled ahead in the alpine valley, finding openings between rigid, dense branches. As I passed over the buried limbs of a great spruce, I fell with my backpack into an immense snow-hole, tumbling upside down, snowshoes on top. I grabbed the shaggy trunk, then plunged my ice axe down for support – but there was none. The snow was over eight feet deep. By grasping boughs I pulled myself up through the needles until my weight was over the snowshoes. Then I climbed back to the surface and slumped over the snow, soaked and exhausted. Fortunately, Chuck was behind and didn't see me.

Rich inquired on the radio, "What is your location?"

I replied, "We're still moving up."

Later Rich called again, "Have you started back yet?"

"Negative."

Disbelief came over the radio.

The weak sun was setting over a bleak Yale ridge and the still air was colder than I'd ever felt. We should turn around, yet I felt a surge of confidence. The Chinook landing was forgotten. I craved to shout in exuberance, but Chuck was such a reserved man.

Every 20 minutes he used the Yagi. When we started up the south-facing slope, the electronic signal became insistent. If a plane had crashed, it was very doubtful that there could be survivors; the lofty elevation, broken terrain and savage weather were too forbidding.

It was now after 3:00 and after talking with base, Chuck followed my deep trail and caught up with me. He reported, "We're the lead team; everybody else was pulled back to base." Only two months in rescue work and I was a front horse.

In base the Civil Air Patrol marked our location and the strengths and directions of Chuck's readings on a map. Horizontal readings increased as we climbed laboriously toward the stormy cirque, a basin formed by an ancient glacier. Snow clouds pushed by a numbing wind began tumbling from the basin to envelop us, obscuring mountain walls that flanked our passage.

The temperature dropped on my thermometer to 20 degrees below zero, but I was overheated and thirsty from too much clothing and the exhausting effort. Fortunately lungs can't freeze, for the nasal passages warm the air as quickly as it is drawn down. Still, feeling the increasing cold of approaching darkness, I didn't remove any layers. My water bottle was filled with ice crystals; I should have carried it inside with the beacon and radio like a trio of falsies.

I told Chuck, "If we're forced to bivouac, I'm prepared."

"No," he said, turning to glance at me. "No, we'll hike out. It would be an unpleasant night."

Rich called on the radio, "You're still going up?"

We broke trail to the edge of the cirque and stood at 11,600 feet in a biting wind that rubbed like sandpaper across my nose and eyes. One mile west across the cirque I saw the stark wall of the Continental Divide. Like a guardian it hung over Kroenke Lake, which slept in the basin under a quilt of ice and snow.

2 way radio

South toward Yale a rounded ridge dropped mysteriously from the obscured 14,194-foot summit, and I scrutinized the rock intently. At our elevation and only half a mile across the valley, an emergency transmitter on that snow-pocked ridge was sending the Yagi a strong signal of 26 milliwatts that came to us horizontally. There was no signal coming to us from above. At our landing zone we had received only three milliwatts, with vertical signals bouncing around and down. Chuck had zeroed in on the source of the cry.

While standing in the snow, we were startled to hear the Chinook plodding up the valley over the spruce, the *whock, whock* of her rotors beating a wonderful rhythm in the lonely twilight. The chopper flew close over our heads. I waved my ice axe and shouted boisterously. In the thunderous blast Chuck motioned for my radio and transmitted to the pilot, "You've come directly over us on the cirque. Can you pick us up in the landing zone below?"

The pilot paused. "I can't wait long. How much time will it take?"

Chuck fired back, "Twenty minutes."

I laughed to myself. We had taken four hours to struggle one mile up; how could we rush back in 20 minutes? Even with the broken trail, it was impossible.

When I slipped the cold radio against my warm chest, Chuck turned, pointed to our tracks, and said, "Baby, we'll have to walk miles off this mountain tonight if that chopper leaves. So move fast!" We never stopped for an instant, except when I stepped one snowshoe on top of the other and crashed over the trail.

After we had come down at least a mile, the pilot radioed anxiously to Chuck, "We have to go, it's getting too dark."

"We're moving fast. Don't go, we'll be there in a minute!"

Soon I heard a steady thunder and found myself peering through the darkness at Captain Ron, a black statue standing beside the white trail. The mercy ship had hovered patiently only a foot over the snow during our hasty retreat.

When I lifted one snowshoe to step up through the side door, the tip caught on the lower step and I fell face down, arms outstretched, into the doorway. I tried to crawl; the crew chief grabbed the pack strapped to my back and hoisted me into the fuselage.

The day's physical effort filled me with a primitive flow of serenity. I'd seen a great mountain in the throes of a winter storm. The pervasive peace I'd felt at treeline carried with me on our flight down North Cottonwood Canyon to Buena Vista. I entered the fire station to find a madhouse. Empty coffee cups were everywhere, the press was questioning any warm body, television cameras stared at searchers, and reporters stood outside freezing in below-zero temperatures for a chance at the only available phone.

That evening Captain Ron briefed us for the next day. "Sixteen of you will take Yagis and fly to the cirque to find wreckage. If you find no survivors, we'll wait until spring to remove bodies. I stress the avalanche danger – nothing is worth the loss of a rescuer." Pressure to locate the emergency transmitter was intense; when its batteries died we would lose the distress signal that would guide us to the crash site.

The next morning was a replay. Up in the dark, breakfast over fires, off to the airport. After the previous strenuous day, followed by a night on a thin pad over unyielding concrete, I had doubts about my performance. The air was cold and clear with snow-burdened clouds crowding against the summits. I calmly watched the Chinook landing. I was an old hand already.

At the cirque raging winds prevented our drop-off. The pilots whirled the aircraft out of the basin, back to the runway.

Our faces were grim, our voices stern. Bruce Bartram, an intense searcher with a charcoal-colored beard from the Rocky Mountain group, growled among the cluster of rescuers, "Is this mission to be scrubbed because nobody wants to do a little work?" Facing Mel, he demanded, "I want to be taken back up there with a strong party of four. I want to be dropped at the landing zone in the meadow. We'll hike up to where Chuck and Peggy were yesterday and then into the cirque."

Mel and Don agreed. The Chinook lifted off and soon dropped through a hole in the clouds that had settled over the meadow. Bruce radioed back, "Keep Peggy in base. We might have trouble finding the route." This was a precaution in case our tracks, which Bruce hoped to follow, had been filled during the night by windblown snow. The Chinook flew all the El Paso folks back to Colorado Springs, with the exception of the "Geriatric Squad," whose members were able to take another day off from work. The press and TV departed in midmorning for Denver. The other groups left for their jobs.

Mel, Dave McMaster and Dick, an Army physician, drove through the snow to a humble cabin at the foot of North Cottonwood Trail where they could relay to base any of Bruce's messages that might transmit poorly across the mountain.

That left three people lingering quietly in the empty bay of the fire station: Stuart Leach, the base coordinator and member of Rocky Mountain Rescue, the engineer with the Civil Air Patrol, and myself.

Bruce and his team reached the cirque only to wage a two-hour fight crossing the deep, fluffy flakes through which thick mountain willow branches penetrated and snagged snowshoes. Yagi readings intermittently radioed to base formed a triangle which the engineer tapped with a pencil. He said to me, "The plane has to be in there."

The sun was low and the radio had been quiet for some time when a voice without emotion, a voice cool and professional, suddenly announced, "Base, we have the wreckage and there are survivors."

Nobody moved. We were stunned. Then, without inhibition, I raised my fist and hollered. Immediately chaos broke out.

Stuart listened to the radio as Bruce identified the four survivors by name, "You say your name is Pat? Steve? And you fellows are Darren and Arnie? We've got four survivors! Send your members back again. We'll need forty of them for the evacuation." As a rule, one victim needs 10 rescuers, regardless of the season; hence the cry for 40. Stuart called on the fire station phone to Colorado rescue groups.

When Bruce radioed their condition from the fuselage, Stuart rushed to the phone again for assistance from Fort Carson. "We need food, water and blankets flown up right now! Can you send us a Huey chopper?"

The good news traveled quickly. In spite of all the vital arrangements Stuart had to make on the phone, reporters from Denver managed to sneak calls through, wanting details which Stuart didn't know or couldn't release yet.

Meanwhile, at the news, Mel, Dick and Dave, in the cabin near North Cottonwood Canyon threw 55-pound packs on their backs and started up the narrow, deep trail, reaching the dark crash site after six hours of snowshoeing. The next day Mel explained to me, "When we'd gone beyond your tracks and into the cirque, the snowshoe trench made by Bruce's team was filled with snow. Even orange flagging markers tied to willow whips were hidden. We were thrashing around in the dark."

Five days earlier, on Christmas Eve, the low-flying white Piper Cherokee, straining to fly just above the trees with only 60 percent of power at 11,600-foot elevation, had banked steeply, caught a spruce trunk with its right wing, and dropped heavily to the snow. Mountain pilots in Colorado know that low air density greatly reduces a light aircraft's performance (the higher they fly, the lower the air density). From a valley they must circle higher and higher – to at least 2,000 feet over the next mountain pass. Then, and only then, they start over. Going for the pass at too low an elevation is disastrous. The plane hasn't the power to climb steeply, and canyon walls may forbid a 180-degree turn.

Unknown to the pilot and four passengers, the emergency locator transmitter was activated by the crash and its signal picked up that day by passing aircraft. The Federal Aviation Administration was notified, and claim they informed the Air Force Rescue Coordination Center at Scott Air Force Base;

but other aircraft traversing the area didn't detect signals, so a search wasn't launched. Two days later other aircraft over-head reported fresh emergency signals to Scott Air Base. Scott requested that the Civil Air Patrol take to the air. CAP pinned the emergency on Mount Columbia. Actually, as we later learned firsthand, the crash site was on Mount Yale, south across North Cottonwood Creek from Columbia.

Photo by Paul H. Swedhin 1982

The crumpled Cherokee languishes on the side of Mount Yale during spring melt.

At the crash site one gas tank, an outer wing section and several tape decks had flown forward and lay on the snow. The intact fuselage became a womb for the passengers during the wrenching days and nights that followed. The survivors in the plane were Texans flying to Aspen for a skiing holiday. The pilot, uninjured, had left to summon help and was miss-ing. Two lanky boys, 15 and 18 years old, their youthful step-mother, and a friend in his 30s huddled in the intact fuselage during gloomy nights that followed days of winds and heavy snowfall. Because they had shipped their heavy clothes separately, they wore only street clothing, but the older boy had packed ski outfits, which they shared. Even so, without food and a stove to melt snow for drinking water, the situa-tion was critical. Eating snow would have dropped their tem-peratures even lower. Food is fuel for the body, and at 11,600 feet in midwinter the furnace needs constant stoking. Without water to drink, their blood would thicken and be unable to enter the capillaries and warm their feet and hands. The two boys, who were able to leave the fuselage, covered a heat-absorbing black briefcase with snow which provided some water. The friend, Steve, ate credit card scrapings of frost from the cabin window. Arnie, the older boy, had packed a Bible, and they sustained each other by reading it during periods of despair. They didn't realize that dense black smoke would rise above burning engine oil or tires and would have been seen below in Buena Vista.

On their fourth day the boys saw our Chinook bank over the landing zone a mile away. Rescue was at hand! All day they waited, but Chuck and I never arrived. Just before dark, the boys heard the chopper circle around the cirque and then down to the landing zone for our pickup. We didn't see them. That night, in acceptance of their fate, they put their lives entirely in God's hands. Steve told a reporter, "The night before we were rescued, I prayed, 'Either let us join You or save us, but please don't let us suffer anymore.' I gave up fighting and put it in His hands."

The youngest, Darren, was near death from the unrelenting cold and lack of food and water. Pat, the boys' stepmother, suffered a severely crushed lumbar vertebra and was in extreme pain. Steve was unconscious for nearly 24 hours from a concussion and a separated shoulder. He was lightly dressed, and frostbite had developed in his legs; eventually both legs had to be amputated below the knee. The boys were frostbitten as well and would eventually lose most of their toes and part of their feet.

The following afternoon Steve remembered Pat reading from the Book of Job. "Just as she finished the part on why God lets us suffer, I looked out the window to see the yellow windbreaker pants of a man snowshoeing toward the plane."

The four rescuers and four survivors wept and celebrated.

"We have some pretty happy people here right now," Bruce radioed. "And they're interested in our water."

The little Huey helicopter from Fort Carson squatted on the runway and loaded supplies. Denver's Channel 7 helicopter had flown over the wreckage during daylight and now led the Army copter through the narrow, twisting, rock-walled route in a highly unusual and dangerous night flight near the ship's maximum altitude.

After the drop of food, water and blankets, the pilots studied a ledge blown clear of snow and dared a landing to bring the victims out. One skid rested on the mountainside, the other perched precariously on top of a rock at a tilt of 15 degrees. The pilots worried. The rotor might strike the cliff and break when they cut power and the blades drooped.

The chopper medic went down to help put Pat on the litter, and the two boys were assisted up, one on a rescuer's back.

Mel, Dick and Dave reached the site. Mel explained, "While we helped Bruce and his team carry Pat six hundred feet up to the chopper, it was dark, bitter cold in the gusts of wind, and exhausting at that elevation. The ridge had been scoured by wind all winter. In some places were six feet of heavy, windblown snow, at other places nothing but loose gravel covered the bare mountainside. When we slipped and tilted the litter, Pat cried out in pain."

At the open window of his aircraft, the pilot, Chief Warrant Officer John Pariury, anxiously waited, watching the storm build over the Continental Divide. He repeatedly looked out the window and pleaded, "I must go, I can't wait any longer, I must go!" Soon the storm pounced down in fury. Despite the bitter cold, Mel saw sweat beaded across the pilot's forehead.

The bird rocked in a 30-knot wind. They slid Pat aboard at 11:00 that night and lifted off in a nose-down angle into heavy snowfall, the rotor straining with seven people aboard. The pilot told me later, "It was the scariest flight I ever made. Stark terror. Worse than Vietnam." The line between fool or hero had been narrowly drawn.

Steve was placed in a sleeping bag and spent his sixth night, with six guests, in the crowded fuselage that tilted forward. The seventh guest bivouacked outside. During the night Steve suffered considerable pain when his frozen legs began to thaw. A blanket of snow over the plane and their cumulative body temperatures brought the cabin air up to about 40 degrees.

News of the mission had gone national, and information was needed. I was promoted from a shy, embarrassed lady to a celebrity because Chuck and I had been near the crash site the previous day. Chuck had returned to his business, and I was left to talk to the press.

At midnight George, a longtime El Paso coordinator who had just arrived, asked me to join him for the 25-mile drive to the Salida hospital to interview the four survivors about the missing pilot. Inside the lighted emergency door I saw Pat's litter adorned with large blobs of snow, which I gathered up and tossed outside. In a nearby room lay the two gaunt youths. The older boy stared at me with dark, sunken eyes which reflected an awareness of death.

George quietly asked the boys, "In what direction did the pilot go when he left the plane?"

A nurse turned and spoke in a cool voice. "I think you should know – the pilot was his father." We had had no idea!

Speaking carefully to Arnie, the older boy, George continued, "Did your father know where he was?"

"We were flying in the rented Piper from Dallas to Aspen for some Christmas skiing. Visibility was good that day, the only day. Daddy thought he was in Independence Pass on his way into Aspen. Before we crashed, Steve told Daddy to find a place to set her down."

The father had been flying only two years, accumulating merely 150 hours of flying time. He had never flown in mountains before and had chosen a risky route, one walled-in by three peaks over 14,000 and restricted by a 12,500-foot pass only a mile west and 900 feet above the crash site. He hadn't filed a flight plan, so was not reported overdue.

"Arnie, do you remember what he was wearing?" questioned George.

"Yeah, cowboy boots, jeans, a leather jacket and my ski hat."

"How much snow fell since the crash?" I wondered.

He turned to his brother. "Two to three feet?"

Darren, limp and moaning on his bed, nodded.

While we were at the hospital, fresh rescuers were spending the night dragging a snow sled up the trail; they arrived at the fuselage at dawn. Steve was tucked inside two sleeping bags and lashed in the sled in readiness for the trek through the basin, into the valley and down the canyon. Forty members from rescue groups all over Colorado worked in teams

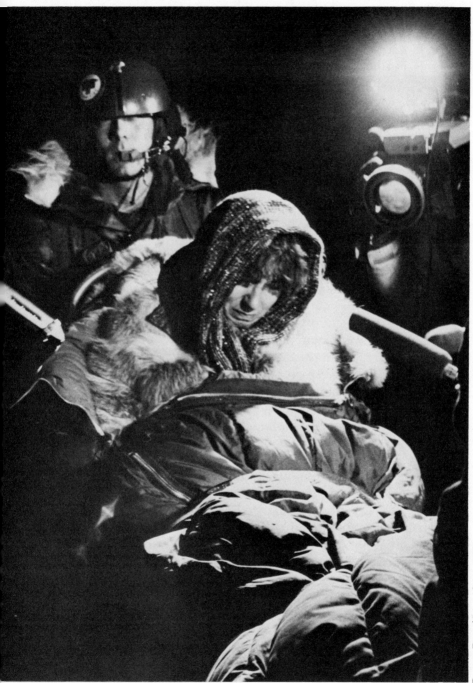

After landing at the Salida hospital, Pat is carried in a litter by a Huey crewmember.

Denver Post / Lyn Alweis 1981

for four miles, using ropes to haul the sled, heavy with Steve, up hills and to brake it on the downslope. The coordinator had had no idea a Huey would carry the three to safety, so the mission had a ratio of 40 to one! Teams, arriving in the middle of the night, started immediately up the trail; several miles up they camped overnight and waited beside the trail as replacements. Once down, snowmobiles dragged the sled two miles more to the roadhead, where the ambulance was waiting.

The day they were due home from the skiing vacation, the day they would be reported missing, the four flew back to Texas from the Salida hospital. Gary, their father, husband and friend, remained alone on the mountain.

The Yale mission was a miracle, but the grief accumulates. The loss of Gary was followed by a related tragedy. In the spring a Fort Carson Huey helicopter ferrying members of a search party looking for Gary crashed and broke in two in heavy timber close to the original site. An Army officer was killed, four were injured.

In early summer as the snow was melting, local teams looked for "reverse" footprints in remaining layers of snow. (A bootprint packs the snow crystals, making it more dense; the print doesn't melt as rapidly as the surrounding loose snow.) But none were found.

Later in the summer when all the snow had melted, Ron, scouting for Gary's body with 22 other volunteers, tramped along the steep mountainside. He told me, "Dense underbrush and rotting timber held us back; logs were at all angles, wet, slippery. I was exhausted at the end of the day. Chances are he'll never be found."

A final attempt was made in the fall to locate the body for the family. This time his bones, clothing and scattered coins were discovered strewn in a small boulder field, and official identification was made from dental records.

Ultimately, Pat had surgery and received a steel pin in her spine. She believes the time spent sitting in the cramped, freezing cabin in severe pain changed her life: "I don't think money or personal belongings are as important as I used to."

Darren spent five months in the hospital, undergoing seven operations in a vain attempt to save some of his toes.

He said, "I figured when we were rescued our feet would thaw out and we'd be able to walk." A persistent bone infection prevented him from regaining his health. He remained in a wheelchair. Arnie, who lost eight of his toes and part of the ball of his right foot, complained, "The loss leaves me nothing to push off with."

Steve moved to a small fishing village on the Gulf of Mexico, where he struggled to master his artificial legs. He said, "It's comical. I take three steps and fall down." He still had to face surgery for his dislocated shoulder.

None of the four had realized the danger in exposing flesh to extreme cold. Severe temperatures cause a limb to turn red. If the exposure continues, the flesh becomes white and numb and will eventually freeze rock-hard. We are told to warm the frozen limb, if possible, in water at 100-105 degrees – only if the limb won't become refrozen. Of course, this procedure is impractical at high elevations. We carry no large thermometer, no large water container, and insufficient fuel to melt snow and maintain the temperature. If the limb is warmed and then refreezes, gangrene may develop. When thawing begins, fluid from the frozen body cells leaks out the ruptured cell walls into leg tissue and stops circulation. A greatly swollen leg results. Sometimes doctors cut through the skin and into the fibrous muscle compartments to relieve this pressure of the swelling on the muscles. With poor blood circulation in the swollen leg, gangrene starts. Actually, a frozen limb hikes better (less damage) than a rewarmed one. Better to hurry him and his still frozen limb to a hospital.

One year later the four still shuddered when they recalled the five days and nights on the mountain. The crash and rescue had appeared on front pages throughout the country, television had beamed out the story of the strong faith of four people, and even today the rescue is discussed with awe.

The survivors filed a lawsuit against the aircraft leasing company alleging negligence in leasing the plane to a pilot who had never done any mountain flying. The company owner said, "I didn't know the pilot planned to fly the single-engine plane over high mountains." An out-of-court settlement gave $375,000 to Pat, the two boys and Steve.

The second summer after the crash, I retraced my steps to the cirque and hiked through the willows to the site. The plane was gone, retrieved by the insurance company. In its place was a brilliant blanket of wild purple asters. I studied a sturdy green Engelmann spruce growing at treeline that bore a deep scar and broken branches where the right wing had struck. A snag tree nearby, a dead patriarch from another century, bore no scar – Gary had flown the plane between both trees in a 30-degree bank.

His invisible bootprints led me east for one-half mile, staying above the spruce, then a turn toward the valley floor for 200 yards, and finally to a small field of boulders from an ancient avalanche. The bitter cold and deep snow had held him there.

I perched on a large boulder and felt a great peace. The warm sunlight falling upon me had become a soft, green shadow in the cool, north-facing woods beyond the rocks. Moss covered the ground and boulders and tree trunks. Huge mushrooms rose out of the moist earth in colors of amber, rust and claret. Massive trees had fallen over during great storms, and their strong roots were exposed and reached for the sky. Bear, elk, deer walked in the woods at dawn and dusk; in midday all was still and peaceful. I sat in silence for an hour, a fitting requiem for Gary, a man who had become part of the primitive earth around me.

3. ALPINE ANTAGONIST

Man is fragile in the alpine wilderness – yet animals, birds and plants survive and multiply in this same harsh environment.

We hastened over the snowpack on the towering mountain face toward a slanting tent, glowing yellow in the chill night. Kneeling at the flap, I thrust my head inside to face the solemn brown eyes of two shivering children, a seven-year-old boy and a nine-year-old girl. They leaned against a young man, who rustled through wet sleeping bags to rouse still another child, a six-year-old boy. Then I noticed an old man lying in the crowded tent. His labored breathing at 13,000 feet alarmed me.

How could this life-threatening situation happen? Too easily. People cannot imagine their own frailty at high elevations. They cannot feel in their minds the harshness of wind and snow and cold when a fast-moving mountain storm blots out the sun's warm rays.

Although chilled and wet, the parents of these young children were able to walk, so the young man, Bob Will – caretaker of Barr Camp, a way-station five miles down the trail – had sent them down the snowfield to a simple A-frame shelter at treeline to build a fire. With our arrival, Bob, who was himself beginning to tremble with cold, left to join the mother and father.

For this mission on Pikes Peak in Colorado's Front Range, we had a team of seven – equipped with ice axes, ropes and two fiberglass snowsleds – to bring down the three children and the old man, who was seriously ill with chronic obstructive pulmonary disease. Only seven members, barely enough, had appeared at the toll gate after hearing the page at twilight. After a year and a half of rescue work, I knew the exhaustion that resulted from too few volunteers. I feared we would be on Pikes Peak all night.

For six weeks this young family, Jo Anne and Kirk, Kyrse, Brian and Joseph, with their friend, 67-year-old Arnie, all from Kansas, had planned a Memorial Day trek down Pikes Peak. Being accustomed to an elevation measured in hundreds of feet, they were lifted effortlessly by cog train to a 14,110-foot summit. The rapid 13,500-foot gain allowed their bodies no chance to adapt to the greatly reduced oxygen. Barr Trail wanders from the summit to the foot of Pikes Peak in Manitou Springs, over 13 easy but long miles, dropping 8,000 feet on the way. The father had visited the peak in years past, but "never saw it so bad." Before starting down, he stood at the summit and "guessed the snow on the face to be a foot deep at most." Actually, three to four feet lay over the trail above treeline.

While walking down the face, melting snow soon soaked the children's sneakers and cotton socks; their feet numbed. The parents tried sliding the children down on their packs, like sleds. The packs fell apart and gear spilled across melting snow. They couldn't continue down, yet they hadn't the strength to climb the 1,000 feet back to the summit and safety. Scattered across the face like their gear, the vulnerable six watched an afternoon storm sweep toward them. Quickly pitching their small tent which had no fly (waterproof cover), they crawled in, carrying the wet gear. The air froze. Four inches of sleet fell out of the cloud to seep through the tent wall and over the huddled figures.

When the storm cloud drifted away, a mountaineer hiking down the face saw their desperate condition. Slogging through wet snow to Barr Camp, he alerted the young caretaker, who hiked up to the tent, arriving just before dark. His emergency radio call brought our rescue team.

Under the haunting eye of a full moon, we loaded Arnie and our two oxygen tanks into a sled. The three children crowded in our warm sleeping bag in the other sled and fell heavily asleep, their heads covered by mops of damp curls. We let down the two snowsleds with countless rope belays, using an ice axe driven into the snow for securing the rope, until we reached a treeline ridge after dawn. There, a Fort Carson Huey piloted by four women soldiers – a pilot, a co-pilot, a crew chief and a medic – lifted the four to a hospital. Conceivably, this crisis could have ended in tragedy if hands and feet and hearts hadn't volunteered after the angry storm. "If those rescuers hadn't come, I really think that would have been the end," said Jo Anne, the relieved wife and mother.

But man is not alone on a mountain. Hardy wild animals, high-flying birds and plants fastened by roots are born, give birth and die on these unsheltered peaks. The amazing alpine flowers on the tundra, tough yet fragile, demand rigorous conditions before they put down roots. With their gentle grace and luminous colors – rich yellows, delicate pinks to rose, sky blues and purity of white – they belong to heaven more than to earth. Like rare jewels, their diminutive size, under an inch, adds a precious value, and in summer I seek them with a passion.

The severity of a summer storm keeps them resilient but low to the ground. Their roots plunge deep for water or to clutch the shifting gravels. They patiently spend the autumn, the winter and the spring smothered under a blanket of frozen crystals. When the blanket melts, exposing leaves to the sun's rays, things move fast. In only a few weeks flowers must open to be pollinated, then the seeds ripen and are scattered over the tundra. Their secret – to set minute flower buds the summer before – is worthy of a higher mind.

What of bighorn sheep – like man, a mammal – who lives above the trees on a bleak tundra ridge swept by squalls? He wears a fur coat but packs no tent. Still, he thrives and raises young. The winter gale that blows across his back also sweeps alpine slopes bare of snow, exposing shriveled grasses and sedges for his grazing – the original freeze-dried food.

Once on a January training class we labored up the cold rocks of Pikes Peak's north ridge, near the summit, when a member exclaimed, "Look! Hikers over there. Impossible!"

"No. Bighorn," we corrected him. This curved-horn sheep can remain above treeline all year, regardless of the weather. He travels on broken ridges and precipitous cliffs for protection from predators – for he's a survivor in all seasons. And during the summer he makes field observations of hiking tourists.

Big Horn Sheep

Not every mammal is above ground through the winter months. In late summer some eat until fat, then sleep until spring. During the worst weather I've ever suffered – an aborted attempt to descend from 14,000 feet on an icy face to search for a lost hiker – I retained my wits enough to muse about some plump marmot, a large squirrel cousin, that was snoozing in protective rocks below my boots. His seven-month sleep, sheltered from the wintry blast, is carrying hibernation too far, I think. Obviously he doesn't. Enclosed in fat layer and fur blanket, he believes, "Why fight the numbing cold? Why not awaken when the midday air is warm?" No wonder a marmot clowns and suns all summer – recess doesn't last long.

For a gregarious marmot to curl up in a dark burrow for over half a year, without eating or drinking or reading a book, and still be alive in late spring, is incredible. But to do this he barely breathes; his body cools and his heart almost stops – a boring state of hypothermia. This true hibernation must be successful for him, for her and for the babies, because the marmot whistle is familiar summer music around rockpiles and alpine meadows throughout the Rockies.

At the same extreme elevation the pika, small cousin to the rabbit, scurries over the snowcover all winter, like the skier, and dines on his summer-gathered haystack. I've not seen him passing the winter in the high country, though I know he's there on his feet because I've read the fact in books. I've listened during our winter practices near tundra rocks for a piercing pika warning, always without success. Maybe the air is too cold for whistling.

During these months of adversity, other mammals, like the pocket gopher, knows life is tolerable in the earth under a snow bank. The ground is unfrozen, a tunnel easy to dig – if one doesn't mind excavating with the teeth and fingernails and pushing soil and rocks around with the chest. By running through his subway, eating roots and bulbs, the pocket gopher avoids the bitter winds and extreme temperatures existing only feet above the tunnels, his underground home. Day or night, winter or summer, life appears the same to this furry engineer.

Instead of sleeping in a burrow like the marmot or running through a dirt tube like the gopher, the snowshoe hare, a loner living just below treeline, embraces winter with zest. I had never seen this relative of the cottontail until a searcher and I were plowing through eight feet of snow on Mount Yale; suddenly he lifted his hand for my atten-

Snowshoe hare

tion. A white rabbit froze only four feet away, camouflaged on the soft flakes. All three of us wore snowshoes – the hare wore two pair. We waited patiently until he relaxed, unfroze, then hopped under spruce branches, leaving goliath-sized tracks. His snowshoes are large hair pads which grow when the air chills and snow clouds blow across the sky. These winter conditions also trigger the growth of a new white suit, which the hare must discard in late spring for a new summer-brown outfit. He's a calendar that hops. Some mammals won't bother primping for snow every winter; instead they go underground.

An animal or bird without a stout heart and strong lungs won't survive at the limit of existence and won't propagate itself. Unfortunate genetic variations in plants are weeded out before the unfit plant can mature and reproduce. Only the adaptable, the fit, survive.

Nature is clever, inventive. Still, all mammals aren't blessed by nature's genius. Man, for one. No thick fur of hollow hairs covers his skin to trap warm air. The sun's ultraviolet rays fry his exposed skin. No down feathers fluff out and insulate his cold-sensitive body. When the air goes too far below zero, his flesh freezes, then dries and shrivels. Should his internal temperature drop only 10 degrees below normal, he becomes comatose and helpless. Let the body stop sweating while exercising in hot air, and heat stroke is rapid. Should his eyes gaze upon sunlit snow, ultraviolet radiation burns them, and the gritty pain and lack of vision immobilizes him for days. High elevation can give man a fierce attack of mountain sickness, even death; at the same altitude, hibernating animals enjoy a reduced heart rate, slowed breathing and the luxury of a deep sleep.

Most of all, man's body is rigid about its oxygen requirements. Ironically, the reduction in atmospheric pressure as man goes higher is also unyielding. As the pressure drops, so does the oxygen content of the air. At 8,000 feet oxygen pressure is 75 percent of sea level – and 8,000 isn't very high. At 18,000 (which is high!) the atmospheric pressure is only half that of sea level, but 18,000 is an elevation out of reach for most people.

Still, in 1978 an amazing alpine ascent took place. Two men, Peter Habeler and Reinhold Messner, climbed to the summit of 29,028-foot Chomolungma (Mount Everest) without supplementary oxygen. Figures from the standard tables show insufficient oxygen for man to survive at that height. But dire predictions didn't come true; both survived.

In 1981 the mystery was solved. The American Medical Research Expedition to Mount Everest discovered that their atmospheric pressure reading on the summit, the first ever, was 17mm higher than predicted. An equatorial bulge – caused by a large mass of cold air in the stratosphere over the equator – caused this higher than normal atmospheric pressure and greater air density. Everest's latitude at 28 degrees N enjoys the effect of this higher atmospheric pressure. And just enough oxygen for rare climbers to make the summit without the aid of oxygen tanks. What a coincidence! Man's elevation limit is exactly the highest point on earth.

When awake at high altitude, man can breathe deeply and more often than normal, to satisfy the demand. The American Medical Research Expedition also learned that some bodies do this naturally, an inherited reflex to low oxygen in the air. The expedition leader, Dr. John B. West, suggests that this response, tested at sea level, might point out who can climb high successfully on major ascent – and who will suffer and fail. When coming from sea level, man should sleep no more than 1,000 feet higher each day when above the 10,000-foot level – to acclimatize gradually, allow his body time to adapt to the reduced oxygen. He should, but often doesn't. When asleep, his breathing rate drops and then trouble begins. With the reduced oxygen comes a severe migrainelike headache plus insomnia and nausea. These dreaded symptoms make him a poor hiker and a dangerous climber the next day.

Sleep isn't a dull and boring state; many vital processes go on in these active night hours. When a climber or trekker or skier is desperate for sleep, the body, craving more oxygen, refuses to behave. Half the night is spent twirling, wide awake, in a confining mummy sleeping bag. Finally, sleep sneaks in, only to be interrupted by an exasperating sleep disturbance, where heavy breathing is followed by 10 to 30 seconds of no breathing. Caused by too little oxygen in the blood, the sleeper awakens suddenly to a feeling of suffocation and panic.

Some doctors recommend various drugs for high-altitude problems. Others are adamant that no medication be taken. Indeed, moving up slowly (or, if ill, coming down fast) is the best pill. The side effects of medication may demand more medication, and that medication may have side effects – and on, and on.

If man takes a traditional sedative to induce sleep, his breathing rate drops even further than is normal in sleep and he becomes even more sick (if that is possible). The day after the sedative he can't think and has poor coordination. He is prone to a climbing accident. The best and cheapest and most available medication for a hiker miserable with common altitude sickness is to stop and fool around for a day. If the misery continues, he should make a 1,000-foot descent; if still no improvement, yet another descent. Just so he descends on his own feet, even in the middle of the night, before he is a litter-case and needs at least four men to carry him off the mountain.

If this "prescription" isn't followed, acute altitude sickness at over 9,000 feet can turn into the uncommon but sometimes fatal pulmonary edema, where the small air sacs in the lungs fill with fluid. Worse still, a rare cerebral edema, swelling of the brain, can develop above 12,000 feet, and is fatal without immediate descent. Himalayan climbers and trekkers know these two edemas all too well.

Alpine-style ascents – a few climbers moving up rapidly – are appearing more often on the world-class mountains. Advocates say serious altitude sickness (pulmonary and cerebral edema) hasn't time to develop. On the other hand, massive expeditions – where the mountain is assaulted by many climbers and endless strings of load-bearing porters – are cumbersome and slow, but allow time for the body to acclimate to the increasingly reduced oxygen. Above 18,000 feet the body has adjusted to low oxygen about as much as it can. Higher can only be worser. This is no problem for hikers in "the lower 48," because California's Mount Whitney in the Sierra Nevada, at 14,495 feet, is the highest. Denali (Mount McKinley) in Alaska's Denali Park, at 20,300 feet, is a different story.

Colorado peak-baggers can develop pulmonary edema, especially the young and eager. Being in superb physical condition doesn't prevent altitude sickness, or pulmonary or cerebral edema. People who are in their mid-30s and 40s or in the grey void beyond are less prone to altitude sickness than robust 20-year-olds, who want the fastest time to the summit and exhaust their energy in the attempt. The older hiker paces himself, knows he will get there eventually. But, alas, age is deterioration. Cells die, lung capacity is reduced and blood vessels become constricted and hardened. Brains don't work as well. The heart beats strangely. But whether young or old, the diabetic, the cardiac, those with high blood pressure or reduced lung capacity, should stay low where the amount of oxygen in the air is ample.

Indeed, mountain search and rescue teams exist because man is tender at high altitude. This fragility was obvious one lovely morning in June when I had been in the group eight months. Jim and Mac, two husky, middle-aged Michigan professors visiting Colorado Springs with their wives for a week,

decided to run along Pike Peak's Barr Trail (the same site featured in this chapter's opening story). Wearing gossamer
shorts and T-shirts, cotton socks and running shoes, they rode
an Incline Lift up to 9,000 feet and then ran four miles to
10,000-foot Barr Camp, arriving in great shape.

"Why don't we go higher?" Jim asked.

When they reached the A-frame, a humble shelter at treeline, Mac said, "That's the summit right up there. Let's go for
it!" The hour was noon. The sun's rays and their running
had kept them warm in the cool air. They had covered seven
miles, not bad for flatlanders. It was only three miles more by
switchback trail across the bleak snow-blotched east face to the
summit, a mere 2,500 feet higher in elevation. Looked so
easy, so close.

After starting up, the two men were fascinated to see a swirling white cloud grow out of the blue sky and obscure the summit. No worry, soon they'd be at the top. When still well below the summit, but too far up to go back to the A-frame, the
cloud, now charcoal-colored, lowered to envelop them in a
wet snow barrage followed by large raindrops, all stirred by a
determined wind. Jim, shaking violently, dropped in exhaustion on a rock – a rock surrounded by forget-me-nots and
alpine primrose, delicate but thriving alpine flowers less than
one inch high.

"I couldn't have gone another ten feet up, or another ten
feet back," Jim told me later. Both men were without food or
warm, waterproof clothing. A passing hiker carried word of
the hypothermic professor and his friend to the summit. The
sheriff's office was radioed. We were paged and drove rapidly
up the 19-mile toll road that switchbacks up the west side of
the peak.

We raced across the summit to the east face and skidded
down a 1,000-foot wet snowfield that overlayed hard ice, until
our team of six came to Jim and his buddy huddled on Barr
Trail. We draped them with layers of warm clothing; nevertheless, Jim continued his uncontrolled and violent shaking.
Our rapid descent had left me overheated. I removed my
outer clothing and slipped under his cover of jackets, to wrap
my arms around his cold chest for an hour. I felt an iciness
ooze out of his core until eventually he and I were one warm
body with two heads. We walked the two men one and a half
miles on the trail to a level bench, where a Chinook flew

through a hole in the cloud and carried professors and rescuers away from the mountain and to a hospital.

This high-elevation rescue of a hypothermic runner caught by a tempest is far too common. But this was a rescue to cherish – later at the hospital the less-frozen of the two professors planted a large kiss on my cheek in gratitude for our efforts. The professors, like most runners, were not delicate men. To the contrary, when warmed, both projected force and vigor. Still, their bare bodies were fragile when wet and exposed to below-freezing gusts.

Had our team not arrived when we did, the core temperature of the shaking professor would have dropped until he lay across the rock in a coma, his metabolism slowed, his oxygen need reduced. One might have said he was "dead." We are taught, however, that "nobody is dead when he's cold and dead. He's dead only when he's warm and dead." When in a deep chill, the body is helpless to rekindle a fire in its own furnace. Then the warmth of a healthy body – skin to skin – is spark and fuel for the hypothermic's recovery.

There is more than hypothermia on the winter mountain. Dick, our physician member, lectures us each winter about watching for small grey spots (mild frostbite) on exposed flesh of the rescuer beside us. In theory, we point out the rescuer's frostbite to him, and he warms it with his bare or gloved hand. (In practice, the rescuer is usually buried under clothing that smothers his skin, even his nose, and goggles that hide his eyes. Only the bulge of a beard gives away his sex, but not his identity).

glacier glasses

In late spring the snow on the slopes lies deep and the sun's ultraviolet rays stab through rarefied air. With the earth's atmosphere thin, no filtering occurs. The hiker or skier bakes in a reflective oven. An overcast sky radiates even more ultraviolet rays. Considering that man can tolerate only a few degrees above and a few degrees below his normal 98.6, a high-elevation tree is extraordinary. I've hiked through limber pine in early morning with below-zero air that paralyzed my face with its sharp edge. In pushing aside a thin branch, I heard to my surprise, the unbending limb crackle – a tree frozen ice-hard. Returning later in the day, after the sun had warmed the pine back to life, I easily tied a half-hitch knot in the pliant branch. I can hardly believe this night-freeze and day-thaw ritual is performed throughout a bitter winter by those spruce and pine and fir that reach for treeline. Many hikes through wind-wrapped crags and across dry outcrops, where alpine trees prefer to make their stand, tell me the winter ritual continues.

High-country trees in Colorado – whether quaking aspen or bristlecone pine or limber pine or Engelmann spruce or subalpine fir – cannot tolerate unlimited cold or unceasing winds. They strive as high as possible, but can't make the summits of 14,000-foot peaks. In Colorado the trees call a halt at around 11,500 feet – some of our rescued folks should have done likewise. This halt in green tree growth is highly visible and is best called treeline or treelimit. Timberline isn't where trees stop growing; rather it refers to a line above which commercial timber isn't produced. Even reaching 11,500 is an admirable feat for a tree, as seen by their intense struggle to survive – for not only one winter but hundreds of winters. A seed germinates in crumbling gravel that blows away to expose roots. A tree spirals the grain of its trunk for strength against cruel winds, winds that sandblast and snowblast. A mature tree suffers bolts of lightning under its bark, often causing an explosion into sapwood. A tree persists on the mountain even after death, standing barkless and branchless, like a ghost that refuses to depart.

Once, on a stormy October day, our team of 42 searchers from several rescue groups took shelter in a sprawling patch of krummholz – the stunted growth of an Engelmann spruce that ventures above treeline. We sat like gnomes between the impenetrable dwarf growths, protected from a steady gale while resting and munching. I feel a deep kinship with these crooked trees, so stately 1,000 feet lower, that crave, like man, to go high on the mountain.

When I was young, I thought a tree grew up the slopes until oxygen became insufficient – I hadn't yet been to Alaska where treeline is close to sea level. Lack of oxygen doesn't hinder a tree, but it sure hampers a man. That was obvious when the midnight crash in January of a single-engine plane on 12,095-foot Independence Pass, just east of Aspen in the Sawatch Range, set off an emergency locator transmitter. The Civil Air Patrol took to the air over the avalanche-prone jagged peak, and at dawn located the wreckage at 13,000 feet. The Beechcraft Bonanza, out of Florida, wasn't destroyed, so survivors were possible. Running hot on the highway with siren and red lights, four of us (all experienced, me with four years) raced to Butts Field at Fort Carson. In one hour a Chinook took us from the airport, at 6,000 feet to 10,000 feet at Leadville for refueling. While there, a ground team arrived at the crash site and radioed our pilots, "No survivors."

The emergency over, the chopper cautiously approached a wide snowfield that draped across a ridge, above the pass. The plane, a small toy against such mountainous grandeur, rested on its wheels, its wings like open arms, only the cockpit shattered. The pilots attempted to land near the victims, but rotor wind threatened to blow the wreckage into the air. They moved downhill a quarter-mile and hovered the bird just over the snowcrust, knowing that if they set down on the snow buried rocks might punch holes in the fuselage.

The pilots warned us, "We only have enough fuel to hover thirty minutes. Don't delay." Evidently they didn't overload for 13,000 feet. That was hardly enough time for a climb to the wreckage and the unbuckling of two bodies – the pilot and his wife – not to mention the dragging of two body bags back over the snowcrust to the Chinook.

The flight crew, our team and two deputy sheriffs from Leadville started quickly for the crash site where the ground team waited. Halfway there the two deputies turned back. I was behind them (I'm a bit slow on uphill). When they came toward me, one walked close to my face and said with emphasis, "How do you do this? I can't make it."

"Well, we're often at this elevation," I exaggerated. Thinking his difficulty might be his age, I smiled and asked, "How old are you?" But, no, I still had nine years on him.

The pace up through breakable crust had affected men acclimated to 10,000 at Leadville. Maybe their legs gave out, or their hearts thumped against their ribs, or the mountain blurred before their eyes. Whatever, 3,000 feet was too much, so they took themselves back to the Chinook.

Was it poor judgment from oxygen starvation that figured into this sea-level pilot's fatal decision to fly at midnight over the winter Rockies? In any case, to fail to file a flight plan in Florida was surely the first mistake of a pilot with only 117 hours of total flying time.

Amid all the research on acute altitude sickness and its life-threatening potential carried out on susceptible man, nobody ever mentions birds. Birds are like some animals in their ability to thrive on the tundra without the ailments of man. Some birds are more winter hardy than the tundra animal who sleeps in a warm burrow or stays awake to hunt incessantly across the frozen tundra. I have read that a bird's body warmth is higher than a mammal's, man's included. I see that a bird's spindly legs, hanging naked in the air, have no flesh to freeze. His bill, too, is of horn, not flesh. I don't notice exposed ears or fleshy tail to harden with frostbite. And his bare feet can stand on icy snow crusts because warm arterial blood, flowing down the legs, heats the cold veinous blood returning – both artery and vein lying against each other.

Even a chicken-sized bird, the ptarmigan, spends his winter on the tundra snowfields, the only bird to do so. He changes, however, to white feathers and lives in wind-protected niches. His hen – they bond for life – sneaks down to spend her winter in the protection of willows at treeline; her idea of Florida.

I was into the study of birds for a few years before joining the rescue team. After such exposure I always had one eye open for a new bird, an old bird or glimpses of their adaptive ways. If necessary I interrupted my participation in a training to briefly pursue a ball of feathers.

Often a mission and a bird fly together. At a mission for Robert, a 12-year-old missing during a drenching June rain on the tundra beside Hallett Peak, in the Front Range of Rocky Mountain National Park, our team was moving slowly over a stream only an inch deep by yards wide that poured from a melting snowfield. Glancing at the snowfield, I was elated to see flocks of brown-capped rosy finches engrossed in eating ice crystals on the snow crust, with water everywhere to drink. How odd! Later I was enlightened. The adaptable finches were dining on a cafeteria of tiny insects blown up from the plains and immobilized on the snow. While observing this fascinating finch dance, the boy we sought was momentarily far from my mind.

The finch migrates high on the tundra only in summer; however, all winter we can observe the raven cavorting with his mate or a friend high in the frozen sky. This classy black bird sleeps in the trees and only patrols high. While up there, he's not feeding or searching for water; he is reveling in the windchill from his soaring speed in the sub-zero air.

The raven is a big fellow, but what of the mountain chicadee – a small nervous body covered with fluffed feathers, the same sleek feathers he wore in summer? He flies through Engelmann spruce at treeline to greet us in wintry air so biting our eyes water. If he doesn't depart the high elevation for the lower prairie, then he lives by his sharp eyes. No seed is safe. Finding a treasure on the frozen ground fallen from a summer grass, he flies to a low twig and, after tucking the seed under his feet, pecks the shell open and consumes the minute morsel. A hiker watches in admiration only feet away.

The white-breasted nuthatch also can stay in the alpine forest all winter, for we see him winging from tree to tree, not far from the chicadee, probing for insects with his toothpick-bill in the crannies of live and dead trees.

A rescue practice or mission on an unsympathetic peak is a humbling experience – frail man has the large brain, but a tiny bird, or a quarter-inch-high forget-me-not, or a 500-year-old tree or a woolly animal is the survivor.

mountain chickadee

4. INNOCENCE

It's the young, who believe they are immortal; the old, who don't realize their depreciation; and the inexperienced, who assume all will be fine – who cause a stream of mountain emergencies.

The September storm, a monstrous thunderhead, was more like an atomic explosion wrapped in black clouds that swept down unexpectedly on an unnamed 10,447-foot mountain in the Gore Range, near Kremmling. Repeated lightning bolts lit the woods to astonishing clarity, followed by blinding darkness that boded ill to isolated, tall trees and grazing wild animals. The roar of hailstones pounding on the forest and the crashing of thunder from above played a deafening staccato, followed by a cold deluge.

On the mountain, Gaile, a lone hunter in camouflage clothing, was stalking elk with a muzzle-loading gun when the great storm unleashed its power. He walked along the ridge to a thick clump of Douglas firs and sat against a tree trunk, protected from the force of the hail. Cross-legged, a cowboy hat on his head, he smoked cigarettes while waiting out the storm. The muzzle-loader bridged his knees, its powder horn in his lap.

When the fury dissipated in the silence of evening, the 44-year-old hunter slumped, motionless, in six inches of hail that covered the soaked earth. His three companions at the hunting camp on Blacktail Creek were not alarmed by his absence during the night, saying, "He'll be back when the hail melts." By noon the hail had melted, but Gaile hadn't walked into camp, forcing the hunters to alert the sheriff.

A private helicopter and fixed-wing aircraft were hired to fly over the terrain, and deputy sheriffs on foot and horseback searched unsuccessfully through the meadows and forest. After three days a statewide call to rescue teams was answered by several groups, and by Ken Cox, a good-natured and humorous airman at the Air Force Academy, and myself, who arrived after 350 miles of pre-dawn driving. In a briefing laced with disbelief, the hunters described Gaile's mysterious absence while we stood restlessly under lodgepole pines, chafing to search the mountain for a stranger from Wisconsin.

His brother, one of the hunters, insisted, "He isn't lost on this mountain. We've hunted here for twenty years."

Gaile's nephew added, "Remember all that lightning? He didn't carry a rain poncho, so hypothermia is possible. Temperatures were in the thirties during the storm."

Hypothermia, a newer word for exposure, is possible when a person's clothing is wet from rain, when the air temperature is cool to cold and when the wind is up. At first the hypothermic person shivers violently, then disorientation sets in, with a dangerous apathy, followed by poor speech, until he becomes semiconscious. A serious situation, indeed.

"Maybe he shot an elk, wounded it and tracked it over unfamiliar ridges," offered a deputy.

"Or he could have slipped in the hail and broken a leg."

We knew every article Gaile carried – candy bars and water, matches, a hunting knife and hacksaw for a captured elk, and his muzzle-loading gun with four loads of powder. We watched for any notes, signs of a recent campfire or crushed grass where he might have bedded down.

The hunters and deputies had done "hasty" searches (a small team moving rapidly over a large area) along Gaile's probable routes for two days before our arrival. Now a "line" search – where members form a line close enough together (in this mission, 100 feet), so that all the terrain is seen – was needed to saturate the ridges and wooded gullies. Sounds simple, but in reality searchers at the end of the line tend to wander off and disappear from sight, while those in the middle move too fast or too slow; then the line is broken and the leader shouts for regrouping. I was chosen a team leader and, despite the exasperations, it was a heady experience for me.

For two days I led a team of eight men through a maze of pines and firs, checking behind buffaloberry bushes, inside alder thickets, under logs. We watched bird behavior for agitation that might signal the presence of a human body, even mistakenly tracking bootprints left by earlier searchers. We called out "Gaile!," then stood in silence to listen for his reply. Shouts of his name echoed between teams and caused confusion.

While we tramped within sight of each other, I reminded them, "Don't let your mind wander, keep alert; other hunters lost or injured have lasted for days."

Late in the fourth day of his disappearance, but my second search day, while scouting along a hunting trail they often used, the brother peered into a fir clump and saw Gaile slumped against a tree, his face and camouflage clothing black from a powder explosion, a cigarette still in his hand. It was the metal in his hatband and gun that had set his destiny.

I believe that Gaile had sneaked under the trees for protection from the hail. He was unaware of the capricious nature of lightning; to be hidden from the sky means nothing to a bolt if an attraction exists. The metal in his hatband and gun attracted a bolt of lightning which struck the tree above Gaile, traveled down the outside of its rain-soaked and rough bark, striking him on the head, then igniting the powder horn in his lap.

Searchers insisted, "We looked carefully for tree damage from the bolt. Didn't see any." Usually a vertical strip of missing bark from treetop to ground is the sign of a strike. Or, less often, the explosion drives a long gash deep into sapwood, leaving firewood-size splinters of wood and bark lying over 50 feet away. When lightning currents reach the ground, either outside or inside the bark, they radiate through the soil and can kill plants, tree roots – or hunters that sit in their path.

Although daylight was dimming, Captain Charlie Carrico, to whom the impossible is possible, had flown over to help in a Fort Carson Huey helicopter and was hovering over-

head. He ordered by radio: Lace him in the litter with webbing. I'll loop and knot a two-hundred-foot rope around the
fuselage, and you tie the other end to the litter. That way
we'll lift him above the forest for the mile back to base. I'll
cut the rope if the litter tangles in a tree. Clear the road of
cars. Turn off headlights, so they won't blind the pilot and
me. When the pilot drops down, get on the radio and call out
the height of the litter above the road."

A critique covering details of the body recovery was held at
base on Gore Pass (9,527 feet). Afterwards, searchers left quickly, for many had a long drive across the state. The hunters
broke down their camp and began a sad return to Wisconsin.

One strike of lightning lasting less than half a second was a
stern reminder of the mountain realities a hunter, fisherman, hiker or climber must reckon with. The dangers of lightning are publicized every summer. Still, many people are
unaware that lightning loves tall objects like trees, or metal
objects like ice axes or rifles.

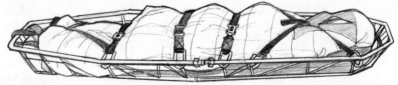

Despite knowing the risks, some people lightheartedly blun-
der through peril, seemingly guarded by a special blessing, an
amulet, that protects them throughout their lifetime. This
shield from harm is often carried by young people, who
believe unending life is reality.

In the warmth of summer this faith in immortality was obvious when a young man, Elias, a sergeant at Fort Carson,
with five years' flying experience at sea level, rented a Cessna
150 one afternoon for "a little sightseeing" in the mountains
with a friend. He didn't realize that horsepower of 150 is in-
suffcient for 10,000-foot mountain cruising in warm, expanded air.

"I began losing altitude over North Cheyenne Canyon,
speeding toward canyon walls, and a downdraft pulled me
toward the ground. I didn't have enough power to climb
over the tight ridges and I was too low to turn." Elias frantically dropped to the trees for a controlled crash. His passenger, busy taking snapshots, was smiling and oblivious of the
sudden decision. To hit a forest, even at a stall speed of 70
mph, is hazardous – like a car hitting a telephone pole. In

this case, the fixed landing gear hooked a tall spruce, which braked the plane's speed and nosed it straight down into the ground, burying its propeller in dirt.

Elias said reverently, "God saved me. If I hadn't given my life to Him, I tell you I'd been a goner." The pilot and passenger hiked three miles to the outskirts of Colorado Springs, and told a strange tale in the early evening.

After nightfall we were sent up the trail that threads through the canyon to locate a victim with wings and tail. In the starlit night the white plane – on its nose, the tail broken – was a fantasy moth illuminated by our probing headlamps. It rested, waiting for a lift from silent rescuers to fly again.

Our leader had told us to sniff for fire danger or fuel leakage into the Colorado Springs water supply. In the four miles of creek that flows from the crash site down to the city's water intake, the fast-flowing stream of cold water would not have filtered out the petroleum. Only warm, still water could do that. Had there been a danger, the city would have immediately closed the shut-off valve until the leakage danger was over.

Fire danger was negligible without a spark to set it off; however, the forester had to cut through the support trees with a chainsaw, in order to drop the aircraft to the ground – in its second crash. In using the chainsaw, a spark might cause fuel to ignite and burn into the surrounding forest. The following morning the timber forester cut down Douglas fir trees in a wide circle around the aircraft to open up a firebreak, before dropping the plane.

To take a chance, crash, climb out uninjured and then credit the good fortune to God, sets a precedent for the years ahead when dangerous exploits will again be attempted, counting on God's intervention to provide a safety net. Yet some people act out entire lives taking chances, testing their luck, only to die in bed at 90, a victim of old age.

My love of adventure began at an early age, during the '20s, in a home that clung to a rocky promontory along the pebbled shore of Long Island Sound. Before I could swim properly I would take a "dare" from three older brothers – scary jumps from a high bridge into a swift current, rides across our millpond on a waterlogged raft, and steps over thinning ice toward open water until the ice cracked. Later, as a stringy teenager living in Southern California and body surfing along the Pacific, I found no ocean wave too high to ride into shore. As a UCLA student, I discovered the stark crags on the Sierra Nevada summits and the purple-hued peaks rising from the desert floor, and I climbed to the highest pinnacles.

On the other hand, those who never flirt with danger can, in their innocence, suddenly suffer a misfortune that robs them of their normal life span. Tony, an 18-year-old, fourth-class Air Force Academy cadet, only three months out of Florida, wasn't experienced in the granite rock found on the Rampart Range that stretches along the western border of the Academy grounds in Colorado Springs. The rounded, smooth tops of many cliffs are dusted with scree – small, scratchy pebbles decomposed from the granite, and waiting to send a man flying.

On a day free of classes Tony left in the cold October dawn, without two companions who reneged at the last moment, to hike around the mountains towering 2,000 feet above his dormitory. Chances are he knew his destination, although the cadets were uncertain of that. We can imagine that he threaded his way through the lower woods with a brisk stride, until the thin air and the abrupt mountainside of the Rampart Range slowed his pace. His steep route was narrowed by cliff remnants, giant gendarmes of stone, that watched him ascend around dry waterfalls and eroded gullies. A roof of pine and spruce branches kept Tony from seeing Eagle Peak summit until the trees thinned and he gazed up at its stern face – a 500-foot wall that overwhelmed yet beckoned him like a seductive nymph.

Maybe Tony had climbed here before and knew both hands were needed, because he laid his duffle bag (containing a Bible with his name inscribed, note pad and pen, box of dry cereal and an Academy handbook) on an outcropping. He fought his way up a precipitous route alongside the massive wall and rested on a rock ledge which rolled away and down the lower face.

He neatly laid his gloves and hat to one side, his shoes to the other, and reveled in the view. Below him the flat-roofed Academy buildings clustered around a chapel that flings its sharply pointed roof up to the sky in bold, piercing projections, like some heavenly space ship waiting for takeoff. On the horizon rested the gentle plains, carpeted with sod and blotched with black drifts of ponderosa pine.

When Tony stood up on the sloping granite flecked with scree, his stockinged feet slipped. He grabbed a pine branch, twisting it off as he fell, bouncing off a ledge, and then dropped to the boulders below. He crawled away, only to collapse on his back and ultimately die.

The tumble was over in a flash. He was alone, no one saw him drop, no one went for help, no one knew where he lay or the moment of his death. His fractured skull and shoulder might not have been fatal; but during the night, below-freezing temperatures and falling snowflakes dealt the coup de grace. When his absence was noted at the 11 o'clock evening check, the sheriff was called; then he alerted us at Search and Rescue.

In early morning a mission leader stood on a table in a field by the Academy fire station and barked a briefing. "We have no idea where Tony went, though some cadets think he headed for Eagle Peak. Maybe so, but teams will also search the nearby mountains and around the reservoir. We've got maps marked with search areas and teams.

Topographical map

We'll use horses and two Huey helicopters to haul you up."

The Huey has only one rotor on top, and, with doors pushed back for rapid entry and exit, exposes the rescuers buckled on the bench. I was dismayed to climb aboard and glance into the cockpit to see a pilot so young he didn't shave. Before I could disembark in anxiety, she turned her face and I saw my first woman Army pilot. We rode this hawk-bird up narrow canyons, alongside cliffs, barely clearing the soft tops of white fir trees.

On the second day Tony's duffle was found, so a team climbed expectantly among the boulders below the face of Eagle Peak. A handler and his dog hiked to the duffle bag from a landing zone, and the handler grumbled later, "My dog wasn't interested in the gear. No scent, I guess. But his short legs gave him fits in the rocks and wash-outs."

A Denver Channel 9 chopper flew Tom Haverty, an engineer carrying a heat-sensitive infrared device, across the mountainside before dawn. Tom detected a "hot spot" below the face of Eagle. This handheld scanning device detects tem-

perature differences of only half a degree Farenheit. Heat radi-
ated from a live or decomposing body would be a sufficient
target. The coordinator told a mixed team of classmates and
Air Force Academy volunteers, "Go back up there. Maybe the
heat this morning was a deer, but there's a chance we missed
him yesterday." They approached from a high shoulder in a
wild and tedious struggle over elephant-size rocks and dangerous drop-offs.

Then an excited voice over the radio, "We've got him!"

Base quietly instructed the rescuer, "Calm down. Approach
the victim slowly, determine his condition."

After several moments of radio silence, the rescuer softly
answered, "Deceased." The squadron commander felt a
"shroud of silence that hung thick in the air."

Perhaps Tony shouldn't have been perched on a ledge that
fell away steeply. One improper step could have sent him
down. Yet ledge-sitting is common in mountains. The
possibility of a slip never occurred to him, since the young
don't reflect on potential accidents; they walk a virgin trail
paved with innocence.

When a young person, one still tethered to his parents, lets
himself slip into a dangerous situation, his intent is often
without guile, his action simply harmless fun. Then the
scene changes. He is sobered to realize what was innocent has
now turned serious. Forced to face adversity for the first time,
the youngster frequently shows a courage, a tenacity, his parents hadn't suspected up to then.

In the spring of my fifth year, I started off one cool evening
with a team of four young Explorer Scouts to hunt for Jeff, an
11-year-old boy. The lad had stormed off toward his cabin in
late morning after a reprimand from a camp counselor. Not
stopping at the cabin, he had disappeared into the steep
woods beside South Cheyenne Creek, west of Colorado
Springs. Mountain slopes are rough there, and broken crags
rise vertically over 100 feet along the creek's waterfalls.

The counselors struck out across the slopes in search of
him. When Jeff hadn't been found by late afternoon, we were
asked to assist. He was a skinny little fellow for his age, with
no rain jacket and no warmth in the cold afternoon rainstorm. He hadn't eaten since breakfast, and now the approaching night became a big worry to all of us.

Just before turning on our headlamps, my radio brought, "We have a Code One." Jeff, numb with cold, was found shuffling toward town along the Old Stage Road that twists its way through the mountains from Cripple Creek.

After cooling his temper, Jeff had realized he was lost, but made his way three miles down the slopes until he reached a private canyon so dramatic in its cliffs that people pay money to enter and gaze. Starting down steep steps that led to the canyon floor, he heard a man shout up at him, "Hey, you. Get out of there!" The man's insensitive shout – another scare added to fright – forced Jeff back up into the canyon, where he persevered through the storm until he stumbled upon Old Stage Road.

Later, when teams returned to the cabin, we found Jeff immersed in a blanket, his appealing face peeking out like a wet chipmunk's, while eating soup from a large bowl. I recalled my childhood in what was then a vast wood behind Westport, Connecticut, where I regularly lost myself on purpose. Secretly, I admired him for his 10-hour journey and respected his doggedness in a growing boyhood.

Sometimes a lost person's survival in an emergency may be jeopardized by some psychological handicap, as well as by innocence. That means double trouble. This occurred when Lance, the 21-year-old son of a family on a picnic, wandered off to explore vertical sandstone slabs that project almost 400 feet into the sky, like giant red cookies set on edge, in the Garden of the Gods, a park west of Colorado Springs. Lance quickly vanished from sight. The family looked frantically for him, but didn't ascend the hazardous rocks.

Our team was called in that early summer evening. When we arrived we had no idea whether he had climbed down elsewhere, or whether he was still up on the slabs, or whether he had fallen from sight. We spread out quickly in small teams – some assigned to ascend the narrow rock passage, Tourist Trap, where he was last seen scrambling. Others of us blanketed nearby rock formations and the meadows below. I glanced over as the light from a setting sunset slowly faded on the rocks, until the sandstone turned black against a French-blue sky.

The searchers who followed Lance's steps up Tourist Trap were peering high among the slabs when, in the darkness, they saw a small flame burning 300 feet away in a level area called Briar Patch, up on the slabs but well below the team. Climbing carefully by headlamp, the team let themselves down to the flame by a 120-foot rope rappel.

The missing son lay among the prickly-stemmed gooseberry bushes that grow on Briar Patch, and into which he had slid and fallen early in the afternoon. In the fall he lost his glasses, and without them he was partially blind. That loss, added to impaired hearing and hip and back injuries from the fall, meant his situation wasn't good. Dragging himself to the edge of Briar Patch, he hung over the 170-foot vertical cliff, and waved for help from tourists standing below admiring the rocks. The tourists waved back.

He waited into the night, the chill and his injuries sending deep shivers through his body, until he heard our people shouting back and forth in the blackness. To attract their attention, he lit his shoelaces with a match. The flicker was quickly seen.

By midnight, the team in Briar Patch, using much rope and muscle, had raised oxygen tanks, a litter, a sleeping bag, technical rock gear and 600 feet of rope. A vertical evacuation (where two rescuers and two ropes, all attached to the litter, are lowered by a brake system) brought a smiling Lance down to an ambulance. His persistence and inventiveness still shone brightly, like two stars.

Similar special situations exist on some searches where the missing person isn't completely responsible for his disappearance. When, one spring afternoon, a mother told her 17-year-old retarded son, Grig, to keep in sight, he decided to "show her." Grig left an obvious trail that led from the west border of the Air Force Academy to small but delightful Stanley Lake, in the Rampart Range, and then took off north going cross-country through wooded slopes punctured by crumbling rock cliffs hundreds of feet high that would menace a mountaineer.

Both parents searched the nearby slopes, patched with snow, and when he wasn't found they alerted the sheriff, who called our search team. In the fading daylight and on into the chilled night, our headlamps bobbed in long search lines under the thin aspen and spruce forest. Dave Bartels, a tall, quiet deputy sheriff and an El Paso member, and his bloodhound, Jessie, joined a team that included Grig's father, to track Grig's occasional prints across the snow. Just before the light of dawn, they lost them.

I came off the mountain long after midnight with a team of 29 from the AFA Prep School. The mother stood waiting for me. Standing in the beam of my headlamp, she demanded, "What are his chances of survival on that mountain?"

"I don't know. I'm not trained to determine chances."

My evasive answer, which in three and a half years I had learned to give many times, was a curtain drawn across the thoughts of his lightweight cotton clothing in the starlit, frozen night, the cliffs and rock slides that endangered his route. I put my arm around her shoulders and stilled the questions with, "The Lord will take care of him tonight." The next morning Grig walked out of the mountain, scratched and shoeless, to a greatly relieved mother who had never stopped asking what his chances were.

During his 20-hour trek, the young man had crossed deep-bedded Goat Camp Creek and emerged near Deadman's Lake. He kept warm by constantly moving, resting only occasionally by leaning against an aspen trunk. After losing his shoes while sliding down a rugged area in the dark, he dropped his trousers to protect his feet when walking over sharp rocks from a rock-fall. He wrapped his sweatshirt around his head for warmth – much heat is lost from the head. On the map as a straight-line distance of four miles, Grig probably wandered over many more than that in his lonely wilderness.

Despite being older, even some parents don't stop to think and learn only by bitter experience. To carry a young boy on the rear of a snowmobile in minus 50 degrees (racing 30 mph in zero degree air) is to chance frostbite on the boy's uncovered face. "Doctor, do you think he'll have permanent damage?" The father asks the emergency-room physician.

"Now, what do you think?" is his scolding reply. The boy's frostbitten face is white, without blood circulation, and hard where ice crystals form between the cells, tearing the cell walls. Frostbite today results in a greater susceptibility to frostbite tomorrow – the blood vessels are permanently damaged.

A seasoned mountaineer recognizes the danger signals; he remembers the circumstances of past accidents and becomes wary of wet rocks, polished surfaces, slippery moss on waterfalls and insufficient clothing. He asks himself, "What if I should fall?" or "What if a storm comes in?" or "Suppose I sprain an ankle?" or "Is it too late to continue up?" and "Do I look good to a lightning bolt?" He realizes that a mountain doesn't go away; if conditions turn bad he can quit and try another day. A knowing climber rises before first light and starts for the mountain slopes just after dawn. He knows the rule: Be off the summit by noon before lightning, hail or rain descend from sudden afternoon clouds that build in a blue sky.

In Colorado we drive through the Rockies, admiring striking rock formations rich in yellow and orange, and soaring canyon cliffs rising majestically hundreds of feet into the air. These intimidate the older folks, who view them with a respect born of experience, but they often entice daring youth to try an ascent. One young fellow, Joe, a professional ice skater, was spending his summer prowling the cliffs of Cheyenne Canyon when Search and Rescue met him. His splendid balance as a skater had allowed him, without training or climbing shoes or technical gear, to climb too far above the ground – and beyond his ability.

The day of our meeting, Joe was slowly climbing 90 feet up and along a wall, a giant rampart rising out of the canyon hillside, while our group across the canyon was practicing setting rescue anchors. To his surprise and alarm Joe reached a point of no return, where his narrow ledge faded out yet he could not retrace his steps. With his toes on the last of the ledge and his fingertips grasping a slight bulge, he gave a continuous scream, "Help, help, help!" which echoed across the canyon.

At breakneck speed we struggled up the eroded slope carrying our rock gear and helmets. I tipped my head back and stared at Joe, his body hugging the wall, and begged members beside me, "Don't anyone ask me to go up there!"

Kevin and Skee, two of our climbers, started up, hammering pitons – metal spikes – into rare cracks in the smooth cliff, for protection from a fall. The lead climber, Skee, needed one hour to reach Joe and wrap webbing around his waist. I sat below with the team, rigid with anxiety, shouting encouragement up. "Don't give up, Joe, hang in there!" By the time Skee reached him, Joe's legs were paralyzed with muscle spasms. Skee lowered him like a sack of grain.

piton

To free-climb 90 feet along a near-vertical cliff of smooth rock, without handholds, to be without a harness and hardware and rope to guard against a slip, is naive and foolhardy. Mel put it well when he said, "We only have to rescue the eager-eyed tourist in tennis shoes climbing for the first time and the super rock-jock climber, who tries too much despite his talents. The staid, cautious fellow in the middle, like me, never gets into trouble."

Many climbers take serious chances. I sheepishly recall a summer in the early '50s when, in a pre-dawn start for the summit of Mount Shasta in Northern California, we confronted a steep snowcrust as hard and smooth as tin. We had foolishly left our crampons behind, with the rope, at camp; but instead of returning for a try at the summit another year, we blithely lined up, taking turns chopping lilliputian steps in the crust with our ice axes, as we tediously moved up the tilted snowfields. Two days later, when we were doing Mount Hood in Oregon, I remembered Shasta and wore my crampons, which shredded my snow-soaked and flapping corduroy pants. After reaching Hood's summit we started down with an ice axe-controlled glissade (sliding over steep snow standing up or sitting down), until my pants and woolen underwear were soaked, their seats gone. I pale to think what would have happened had a severe storm suddenly raced in from the Pacific. By reminiscing over my past, I hope to understand our victims today.

Certain others we are called upon to rescue are not so much unaware as they are unacceptable – "losers," people who by their actions are always getting into trouble. As a prelude to disaster, this type often flood themselves with beer and take a spin through mountains on narrow roads, snaking above slopes that drop hundreds of feet to trees or rocks below. The scenario is familiar: an emergency call after midnight, a dash into the mountains, the flashing red, blue and white lights at the scene. A sheriff's deputy points down a beam of light in the darkness, and I see a crumpled car, a toppled tree and a paramedic bending over a prostrate body.

At one such mission a rescuer asked, "Do you suppose he was drunk?"

In a patient voice, Dick, our physician member, answered, "Now how do you suppose he got down there?"

We bring the victim to the road above in an "uphaul" system (using a pulley and a 200-foot or more length of rope) requiring at least eight from our team, and I long to say to the litter occupant, "Hey, old boy, drink in bed, safe from harm." One passenger in a Fourth of July incident was so fortified with booze that the paramedic radioed the hospital for permission to add morphine as pain relief for his fractured foot. Alcohol and morphine both dilate the capillaries, veins and arteries, reducing the amount of blood being pumped through the heart and resulting in a severely lowered blood pressure.

Team members never openly judge victims or the actions that cause their trouble, but, privately, I do. Nevertheless, we must take it the way we find it, and then, somehow, deal with it. I ask myself, "Who will get them up, get them down or find them, if not us?"

I've made many innocent mistakes myself. And I've also taken chances fully aware of what I was doing. Looking back once again to the early '50s, I recall the little band of men with whom I hiked to Sierra summits. One, an obstetrician – who later introduced me to my husband – asked us after an amateurish free-climb that demanded rope protection from a fall, "Want me to get a library book on climbing, buy a rope and a couple of carabiners, so we can learn this rope climbing stuff?"

"Sure, why not?" we answered.

Descending devices weren't around then, so we used a dulfersitz, or body wrap, to rappel down a cliff, the rope often burning into shoulders something fierce. We had never heard of webbing and had never tied into an anchor; more than once my derriere was dragged along a rock surface by a heavy man rappelling down the rope wrapped behind my waist. We belayed climbers in the same unsafe manner, and could have been jerked off had our climber lost his grip and fallen. Such casual technique is embarrassing to remember, and that we all survived is quite remarkable.

Thirty years later and a new rescue member, I was still unconsciously testing my luck, allowing my eagerness for a mission, any mission, to override my lack of experience in rescue work. My first mission soon after joining was almost a calamity. A young man, Arne, had been walking across the rounded top of Silver Cascade Falls in North Cheyenne Canyon, when he paused for a cool drink. Green moss growing in water flowing over the rock was slippery, and he took a long fall to the first ledge, fracturing his hip.

An emergency call went out. Living close by, I was the first rescuer to appear beside the waterfall. Before walking across the sharply tilted rock face, I paused to put on my helmet, which belonged to my son. I'd never worn it. While spectators stared, I tried to determine the front from the back and where to put my skull through the confusing straps. I tried repeatedly, finally gave up, stuffed it in my pack, and gingerly crossed the smooth face without it. My maiden mission had begun and already I was acting strange.

When Skee, our member in charge, appeared, I exclaimed, "Am I glad to see you!"

Only five people could fit on the ledge where Arne lay, soaked and cold, his pants unzipped to expose the swelling hip. I feared one of the arriving firemen or police officers would tell me to leave so he could take my place. I wanted to be involved in assembling the litter halves, in placing Arne in the litter and in carrying the litter.

Leaning over Skee's back, I whispered, "Don't forget, I had litter training this morning." Ten minutes' worth.

Without turning, he quietly ordered, "Get your harness on. Your helmet, too."

I discovered that the harness needed to tie me to the litter was in my truck. Someone tossed me some webbing, which I wrapped around my waist and knotted, as my hands shook uncontrollably. Worse was yet to come. One end of a 200-foot nylon rope was tied to a sturdy ponderosa pine high above the falls, and the other end to the litter beside the falls. Skee

harness in use

explained, "Now we'll lift the litter and lean back, facing up-hill, to get the stretch out of the rope." I was alarmed to feel Arne's weight. He was over 200 pounds. What would the guys say if I let go? My webbing was too long and I couldn't lean back to let my weight hold up the litter; instead I took the weight in my arm and shoul-der. It was too late to adjust. When the rope stretched 10 feet (with the weight of Arne, four litter-bearers and the litter), the litter extended beyond the shelf and out over the waterfall. I was left hanging backwards in space, my feet braced against the steep rock wall. With screaming muscles, I bent over the litter and hung on, while trying to hold up my share of Arne as we pendulumed across the waterfall successfully. A tidal wave of relief washed over me. I hadn't fallen down.

My weaknesses – macho inclinations, forgetfulness, trem-bling hands – must cease. During the five years since that first mission only the trembling hands have vanished.

5. THE CHINOOK AFFAIR

To the hunter or the climber or the hiker in distress,
a Chinook and its penetrator hooked to a steel cable
is a wingless angel on a flight of mercy.

 "If you touch the penetrator before it hits the ground, two thousand volts of static electricity will scare the fire out of you," Captain Charlie snapped at us. Fire out of me? Was I the only member trembling while the helicopter approached?

"And if the cable unwinds or swings, don't throw up over the penetrator." How revolting!

"Finally, when crewmen pull you off the penetrator, don't fall through the cargo hatch." For a 100-foot drop to the ground? Hardly.

Captain Charlie – his mustache and hair the color of corn, making him look half his age – stressed each alarming instruction for riding up to, or down from, a Chinook in flight, as we watched the prehistoric monster skim over the grassy fields and wooden Army buildings at Fort Carson. I had been a member a year and had faced many a challenge. This was something else. My stomach told me to run, but the team would know why. I must stay and fight this fear – not of heights, only of dangling in the air below a cargo hatch.

The penetrator, a bullet-shaped contraption three feet long, was used in Vietnam to rescue soldiers from the jungle. It hangs from a hook at the end of the 120-foot hoist, a steel  cable attached to the aircraft. Three projections open out from the penetrator, like petals on a daisy. I was to drape my legs over two of the petals, fasten a strap around my back, and clutch the cable. Then be lifted slowly to the cargo hatch. Sounded safe. The Chinook's twin rotors revolve to hold a steady hover at 100 feet – but, should power fail, the clumsy insect would fall to earth and squash me like a snail under a gardener's boot.

My entry was to be the 4-by-4-foot doorway in the belly of the ship. Unfortunately, the cable stops below the gaping hole – better for hauling cargo – so a crewman would lean down and out and tug me up into the fuselage. For a fearsome moment I would be neither attached to the penetrator nor safely in the aircraft. Crewmen always wear a harness clipped to the fuselage; I planned to grab my crewman's leg with a stranglehold.

"This is good practice for the helicopter crew, they're new at it," I overheard Captain Charlie comment to a colonel watching nearby. I hoped the two pilots had flown their aircraft before.

I knew the crew chief watches down the hatch and regulates speed by a cable-hoist control in his hand. Should the cable tangle in a tree and endanger the chopper, the crew chief fires a .45-caliber cartridge that drives a cutting blade through. Farewell to penetrator and rider.

This nightmare of instructions ended and practice began. Our chopper, its motors howling and rotors beating the air, hung above the field. A lieutenant rode up first and disappeared into the hole. I watched intently without breathing, my mouth like the Sahara. If I was going to ride the darn contraption, I must do so quickly, before trembling hands got worse. I signaled my willingness to go next. As the penetrator was lowered on the cable, I ran into the rotor wash. When my legs were hooked over the petals and the strap was across my back, I threw an arm into the air with a thumb up. I slowly rose like cargo to the belly of the massive ship. Then something wonderful happened – I felt no fear, only great excitement. Although battered by the rotor wind, I peered down to see our team shrinking and glanced up to note the beast enlarging.

Suddenly a crewman crooked his hands under my arms and attempted to lift me backwards into the fuselage. To take leave of the penetrator and trust a strange man to keep his grip was too much. I looked for his leg. On his second tug I sprawled across the metal floor and realized the leg-grabbing time was over.

That joyous but always dangerous ascent has been repeated often, up and down, solo or sitting on another team member's legs, always without problems. I became impressed with myself, forgetting that practices are easier than missions. Yet during missions, men are always chosen to ride the penetrator. During my first three years in rescue work, I was hoping such favoritism would change; however, it never did. Then a rescue came along that forever cooled my passion.

I recall the problem as a broken leg between two waterfalls on Mount Shavano, in the Sawatch Range, a fourteener (a peak over 14,000 feet in elevation) near Salida. Although not in our county, we had been requested to give assistance. While racing through the night to the mountain, dodging aimless deer in the road, we received a radio call. "We are completing the rescue. Won't need you. Thanks for responding." Our rescue vehicle, loaded with gear and members, swung back toward Colorado Springs.

The next dawn a page went out asking for members to act as observers on a Chinook that would return to Shavano. The victim's girlfriend, who had been thrown a blanket but left at the scene for the night, was now missing. I was unfamiliar with the area but wondered why they didn't look around; she couldn't be far. Regardless, I never refuse a Chinook ride. Pushing aside my work, I dashed to the aircraft and discovered that Rich, an electrical engineer, and I were the only rescue members aboard.

Mount Shavano, although impressive at 14,229 feet, appears benign. Three deep and long crevices high on the slopes remain filled with snow in late spring and most of the sum-

mer, in the shape of a benevolent angel with arms outstretched – the famous Angel of Shavano. Numerous gold
and silver mines that were bored into the summit crest at the
end of the last century are less romantic. Our ship wandered
around some ridges and then started down a canyon that
opened my eyes wide. The canyon floor was one continuous
slab of polished rock that lay almost vertically against the
mountainside. A rushing stream poured over the rock, falling 80 feet to a ledge, then another waterfall, and another
ledge. And, no doubt, more waterfalls beyond my sight. Earth-
en walls, encrusted with trees, rose steeply beside the aircraft
only to disappear in the sky above.

The canyon was too tight for the ship. Nevertheless, the
pilot dropped lower, and still lower, until spruce and fir
branches were gesticulating wildly in the rotor blast just outside my window. Everything inside me sped up – blood pressure, heart rate, palm sweat. I was strapped in the fuselage, no
chance to fight or flee.

The crew spotted searchers between waterfalls, but the team
leader carried no aircraft radio. Not all search teams have aircraft contact, yet where a helicopter is involved, carrying one
should be de rigueur. Someone had to descend on the penetrator to learn if the missing hiker had been found. The cargo
hatch was opened and a young sergeant aboard hopped on
two petals and disappeared. Our pilots sat stiffly in their seats,
one holding a tricky hover. A dead tree crowded in front of
their cockpit. Behind the tree a palisade of wet rock limited
our escape to straight up or straight back. Within moments
the sergeant hung once again in the hatch, and I saw a woman sitting across his legs. A crewman yanked her into the
aircraft and pointed to me. I showed her a seat belt next to me
and held out earplugs.

"Are you injured?" I shouted.

"No!" she insisted.

Then why couldn't this woman, the missing friend, walk
out with rescuers on the ground? Mysterious. Later, out of earshot of the woman, I chided the sergeant. "That was damned
dangerous. Why'd you bring her up?"

"I got those pilots up early this morning; someone was coming out," he whispered, and we chuckled over his secret.

Although it aged me, the mission had been great practice,
like a training maneuver, for pilots and crew, and a worthy

challenge to their skills. A Chinook is flown by two pilots, in this case Vietnam veterans, and several crew members, all of whom exude assurance, almost a boldness. To them danger is a companion, not a foe. What may look perilous to the untrained may be old hat to the professional.

Dick, Peggy, Mel and Ken , along with other rescuers, return from a mission.

That canyon cured me of any zeal to ride the penetrator on a mission, and temporarily cooled me to the Chinook. The concern I felt wasn't that a rotor could strike a tree, causing us to crash on the waterfalls, but rather that if I rode the penetrator and it snagged a tree and threatened the aircraft, the crew chief would discharge the cable-cutting blade. My worry was wasted emotion; the crew didn't invite me onto the contraption.

Then, two years after Shavano, my love affair with penetrator and hoist suddenly ended once and for all. Bob Sheldon, a new rescuer in his 20s from Grand County Search and Rescue, fell 25 feet to the ground when the hook and its cable separated in his first ride. I didn't see the accident, but reports of fractures to both his arms and both his legs devastated me – to this day I feel that I may never perch on a penetrator again.

To ride a penetrator is one of three ways to leave a hovering Chinook. Another is to simply jump out into space, a distance I have never seen to be more than eight feet. Another possibility is to tie a rope inside the fuselage and rappel off the open ramp to the ground, assuming the rope reaches the ground. To rappel, the rescuer passes the rope through a friction device attached to his harness, or gains friction by wrapping the rope in a certain manner around his body, and then descends, sliding the lower section of the rope through his gloved hand as a brake; this friction produces a controlled drop – and a hot paw.

Once, in my second summer with the group, I was in Ridgway (north of Ouray) in the San Juan Range for a practice with other state rescue teams. The view to the south from the chopper flying over grassy meadows is perhaps the most spectacular in Colorado. Mount Sneffels, the only fourteener close by and a peak not smoothed by the immense Pleistocene ice cap that covered the area, is made of hardened molten rock. It dominates a tight necklace of 13 jagged and pointed peaks, all just under 14,000 feet. But that morning these clustered mountains and the warm sunshine falling on us must have anesthetized me, for when Captain Charlie asked for volunteers to demonstrate the rappel from the hovering Chinook, I raised my hand, along with four men. I'd never rappelled from a hovering chopper before. Rescuers would watch from a meadow – which is where I belonged. I'd forgotten who I was.

A lieutenant briefed us. "When you go into your 'L' position and drop into the air, be careful not to crash into the ramp with your head." A crewman was taping a thick carpet on the ramp edge for the practice. My helmet and their carpet – some duo to protect my skull.

"Don't go upside down, don't panic and don't grab the rope with both hands," he continued. His words echoed inside me.

"Skee smacked his head the first time he tried it," a friend offered. Skee was a monkey on rope.

A deep breath cleared my head. I was a woman and too old for heroics. Anyway, during a mission I wouldn't be asked to rappel out of a Chinook. So just cancel. Whisper to the lieutenant. The group won't know.

Before I got the lieutenant's ear, a pickup bounced over the pasture and carried Captain Charlie away for a phone call. Soon he returned and hurried to the aircraft.

"Must be important. Charlie never runs," an irreverent crewman remarked.

Breathing heavily, the captain ordered, "Everyone out except El Paso. Get your gear fast. We have a mission."

I ran for my gear. The taped carpet was ripped off. And the pilots started the motors. How fortunate. Now teams would never know I couldn't rappel, that I was scared.

Captain Charlie said our mission was for Bill, a 58-year-old geologist hiking with his family. He had had a possible heart attack and a severe head injury from a fall, and now lay just below the 14,267-foot summit of Torreys Peak, in the Front Range west of Denver. While refueling at Grand Junction, our leader, Ron, said, "We'll have to hurry. CPR has been going on for an hour. A team will rappel from the aircraft to the summit." He called out the team – I heard my name. Fear at Ouray now became terror at Torreys.

We left Grand Junction, on the western slope, for the Continental Divide, climbing through cobweb clouds while wipers swept raindrops from the cockpit window.

I sat belted on a bench, my mind stuck in first gear. The possibilities were too horrible to contemplate. How was I to rappel without my head cracking against the ramp, a ramp now without a carpet? What would I do if the pilot couldn't hover precisely over the ridge, or if my rope was too short?

The ride through the storm was rough, full of jolts and sinks, but I took no notice until our youngest member, sitting next to me, shouted into my helmet, "I'm sick!" Vomiting over the floor is verboten in a Chinook, because the acid from the stomach eats into the aircraft frame; floor plates must be taken up and the area cleaned. I moved away from him as far as my seat belt would allow while signaling the crewchief for a plastic bag, which arrived barely in time. I covered my eyes.

We landed below the mountain in a dirt field at little Bakerville, about 60 miles from Denver, where an ambulance was standing by. From the frontage road off Interstate 70, I looked up to see the shoulders and summit of Torreys. While we were swiftly working under whirling rotors to empty the fuselage of unnecessary weight, a woman in a paramedic's uniform entered the front door. Nobody, not even a paramedic, enters a Chinook without being invited. Stunned, we stared at her. Neither the crew chief nor Captain Charlie had invited her aboard, especially through the front door.

"I'll ride up with you to the victim," she explained.

"You'll get your ass off this aircraft," Captain Charlie replied, in a voice that would have soured milk.

Within moments radio word came from the Alpine Rescue Team on the mountain that the climber was dead. The team had raced up the steep trail, carrying heavy oxygen tanks. Bill Butler, an Alpine Team member and emergency medical technician, couldn't get a pulse even with a stethoscope. The family, inexperienced, had been attempting to take his pulse with a thumb, instead of a finger, and succeeded in taking their own pulse. I grieved for him and the family, but at the same time I felt a sudden release from my stress over the rappel.

The Chinook, emptied of gear and with only three members and one crewman, accompanied the two pilots to the body recovery at 14,000 feet. The rest of us, including Captain Charlie, remained on the ground in Bakerville, proudly watching the black ship turn to silver, as the fuselage reflected the glow from a setting sun.

Vivid pink smoke, from a cannister popped by Captain Charlie for wind direction, guided the aircraft to a blocked-off road. As we unloaded the Chinook, my throat tightened when I glanced at the comfortable and well-used hiking boots the climber had worn to scale Torreys, his favorite peak. Later, when the autopsy was completed, we learned that death was from a heart attack, not from the tumble that followed.

That afternoon I had been possessed by a haunting fear of the ramp rappel, yet our team never mentioned or practiced – much less used on a mission – the technique again. Perhaps this hidden terror remains my private humility.

Chinook helicopter

As helicopters go, a Chinook is no swan. The aircraft, a CH-47C, is the most Neanderthal of flying machines. Designed for function only, its boxy body is beautiful in its efficiency – its ability to move troops, transport cargo and haul a rescue team to 14,000 feet. To stand on the ground and look overhead to see the aircraft slowly propelling its beetlelike body forward by two spidery spinners revolving in opposite directions, is to marvel at the miracle of flight.

My devotion to this flying creature is boundless. This passion is more like the love of a mother cockroach for its baby – I see only its virtues, not its appearance. After countless rides in its smelly and noisy fuselage, I can't recall the color of its outer skin – brown, black or Army green? Yet I know the scarlet-red canvas seats that drop from the fuselage wall. My ears still hear an echo of the *whock, whock* that comes from the massive twin engines. Now I close my eyes and trace the exposed bundles of colorful wire and aluminum tubing that wallpaper the inside of the skin and carry jet fuel, hydraulic fluid, electricity and oxygen from front to rear. Or is it rear to front? I no longer look for rudders, elevators or wings, for I know the rotating blades and their variable pitch do all the flying.

To have aircraft guts in full view of passengers is fascinating but disconcerting – so much can go wrong. Worse still, a rescuer can hang out the front door and look back along the fuselage to note the paper-thin aluminum-magnesium alloy skin that wrinkles and bends on lift-off. It shouldn't be a problem, since the skin is riveted to the skeleton shaping the fuselage. Or does that mean the skeleton is buckling? I remember the day a pilot showed me how to exit the fuselage after a crash by chopping through the skin with an axe. Pilots and crew chiefs talk too much about "after a crash."

A Chinook has power – the power of 7,500 horses – and maneuverability that other helicopters and fixed wings don't have. In a war it extracts crashed aircraft and sling-loads them away. On our searches for missing planes along the snow-burdened shoulders of big peaks, we can signal the crew to go into a couloir and study a suspicious pile of buried rock. The pilot stops, backs up the aircraft like a truck on the highway, swings into the couloir and hangs motionless for minutes in the rarefied air before turning around and moving out. Most impressive! And a change in one flying procedure doesn't require adjustment in two others, as in other flying machines. In the eyes of one pilot, Chief Warrent Officer Lynn Larsen, "A Chinook is the Cadillac; all the rest are Volkswagens."

Of all its peculiarities and wonders, the flexible 60-foot-diameter rotors, drooping like antennae on a melancholy insect, seem the strangest. At rest, the front fiberglass blades hang to four feet, four inches off the ground – beheading at the waist becomes a possibility. In fact, head-removal by any of the six blades on the two rotors takes only a second of inattention, especially on mountainous slopes that rise under the rotors.

I watch crewmen like a hawk. In brief landings during a mission one always climbs up the fuselage to study the rotor transmission, another will squat down to study the belly of the old beast. I crave to ask, "Is something wrong?" On one flight I watched a crewman use pieces of wire to replace two motor-mount bolts that fell out from the vibration. The embarrassed crewman ignored the 20 rescuers studying his every move. When fuses blow, as they do, our flight is delayed 30 minutes; a cumbersome toolbox is wheeled toward the cockpit and replacement occurs. Lift-off follows with the crewman belted on his red canvas seat, proud and protective of his aged machine.

The Chinook, workhorse of the Vietnam War, was born in 1961, and its production was stopped in 1970. Now in the mid '80s, the classic box is acquiring a face-lift, a strip job to the skeleton, with fresh skin and mechanical parts for it to wear for future decades of flying.

A rescuer can't be timid on a mission, although most experience brief moments without courage. I know Chinook rotors snap off in severe turbulence, but then avalanches scoop up rescuers and freeze them to death, and overly stressed ropes have been known to fray and break. My antidote to these fears is to take the risk and confront death head-on.

In my early years in rescue I was extremely conscious of the rotating wings overhead and was bemused when a crewman used a cable to tie each blade to the ground at nightfall, like hobbling a horse. Now I know the honeycombed blades, reinforced by a titanium strip, will flex to the sky in an alarming fashion during a gale on the runway. Where the three blades join in the center of the rotor, there is a round hole that slips over the shaft and a "Jesus-nut" holds the rotor down tightly. The name has religious overtones because if the nut comes off, "Jesus, you're dead."

To date I haven't seen a female in a Chinook cockpit, but I'm told there are several. Why not? Women fly a Huey with grace and dash. To my joy, a rosy-cheeked woman grasping pliers and wearing a mechanic's suit was scrambling over a Chinook fuselage with the men at the airfield one recent afternoon.

When this bizarre bird lifts off, the front end rises first; after a pause, the rear follows, like an afterthought. Coming down to land, the technique is reversed; the pilot sets down the rear, and if all goes well he drops himself. Coming down over deep snow is tricky, at best, for the pilots are blinded in a 125 mph blizzard stirred up by the front rotor. By dropping slowly from an elevation of 150 feet, however, the front rotor will blow away all the loose flakes, and the pilot can look out and see a reference point for hovering.

altimeter

The aircraft is amphibious and will float indefinitely, like a frog, provided the bilge pump in the fuselage is draining any water leakage. With no pump, the 15-ton ship gurgles to the bottom in 30 minutes, just time for the crew to take to the sea. Safety features abound: an axe hangs on the wall for chopping a way out; and the six fuel bladders, holding 7,000 pounds of jet fuel, will self-seal if punctured by an ice axe, or will separate from the fuselage in a hard landing – also known as a crash.

To my mind, the most critical safety item is a state-of-the-art oxygen mask, worn over the pilot's nose and mouth, with a radio mike buried inside. If oxygen will be needed, the pilots must use the mask before they "suck air," as they say. For without sufficient oxygen in the blood of our pilot or copilot, we rescuers belted on the fuselage benches are being flown by a brain suffering from confusion, memory loss and dizziness – a lack of mental sharpness. Actually, only two Army bases have oxygen installed in their Chinooks – Fort Carson, with a ceiling of 15,000 feet, to cover Pikes Peak, and Alaska, with a 21,000-foot ceiling, to make the Denali summit.

"You know, Peggy," said Mr. Larsen, a long-time pilot and chief warrant officer, "In the beginning we pilots poked a hole in a surgeon's mask, stuck in a tube carrying oxygen and just opened the valve. We had no gauge to give us the rate of flow." We laughed heartily at their casual behavior.

One afternoon in talking with the pilots, I felt their love for the aircraft; their personal commitment was made clear when Chief Warrent Officer Charles Davidson said simply, "We take a great sense of pride in our missions."

"Yes," Mr. Larsen agreed.

In the moment of silence while I took that in, Mr. Larsen added humbly, "I've done forty-nine people rescues – twenty-five have been live."

I look back on my chat with the men and contrast my behavior with their behavior. I tend to come across like some wild-eyed cow escaped from the Adrenaline Ranch, while these pilots speak slowly, carefully. The words are soft and flow with confidence from someone who knows hairy mountain landings and dangerous rock cliffs, and who has felt violent downdrafts wrestle with his flexible rotor blades.

Although rescuers, who appear regularly at fly-away missions, soon become acquainted with the various Chinook pilots, one military man in particular – the flight commander – stands out as our ally and friend. Never speaking while in flight because of rotor thunder and ear plugs, the commander merely lifts his hands to indicate, "Depart the aircraft fast!!"

In my five years I've seen our members leap to the signals of three commanders, with a few in between on temporary duty. Their absolute ways were always accompanied by a rare wit and a deep kindness toward victims.

The first commander I faced was Ron Liss, a captain who was never rattled or grumpy, and in my eyes, stood taller than his considerable height. His finest trait was his acceptance of me as a young charger – one wearing a wrinkled overcoat.

No one could turn him aside or talk him down. I look back on one night in the Buena Vista fire station during a plane crash mission, when Captain Ron demanded another Chinook from a Fort Carson colonel for the Crested Butte search for a cross-country skier. The colonel refused. In a thunderous voice, Captain Ron roared into the poor phone, "Are you trying to tell me how to do my job?" Aghast over his words to a colonel, I slid to the bottom of my mummy bag.

When Captain Ron, flying with our team on the final mission under his command, introduced his replacement, Captain Charlie Carrico, to me, we stood in a moonless midnight and shook hands by the aircraft, darkened to preserve night vision. Minutes later, while entering the high, oil-slick ramp, I caught my boot sole on the edge. The weight of my pack caused me to fall on my stomach. In the dark nobody saw me. I got up, replaced the heavy pack on my shoulder and stepped forward – the same toe caught again, down I went. Sighing, I tried once more. Incredibly, the comic scene repeated a third time. While down, someone grabbed my britches and pack and lifted me onto the ramp. Since then Captain Charlie, my deliverer, says to everyone, "When I first met Peggy, she fell three times getting into the helicopter."

With his priceless remarks, straight out of Texas, Captain Charlie was a constant joy and an insufferable tease. He made outrageous remarks to women – the kind they love to hear. When we were firm friends he referred to me as a "pterodactyl," thanks, no doubt, to my similarity to the flying reptile, now extinct.

Nothing daunted Captain Charlie. When a Chinook in which he was commander was unable to land and drop off a search team in Beaver Creek Gorge, he grabbed an axe, hooked the penetrator onto the hoist and rode to the ground. There he chopped down the cottonwood tree that prevented landing of the ship.

Captain Charlie was born 40 some years ago in Deadwood, Texas, making the population, in all, 19 people. The closest town was Bobo with even fewer people. When a tad too young, at 15, this Texas toughie joined to fight a war.

Captain Charlie retired with his wife and son to Monument, 20 miles north of Colorado Springs, "to a log cabin I built myself in a wooded valley all my own." With a pension, he doesn't need to rise with the clock; regardless, he reports in as an ambulance paramedic for work days that last 24 hours. He says to me, "I get a lot of gratification out of it." One of his partners on the ambulance described him with the right word – a romanticist. But he is always Captain Charlie. One day we met in a crowded emergency room. After a big hug, he ran his fingers down my spine and announced to all, "You're still not wearing a bra!"

I tagged along in his ambulance one summer Saturday, trying to come upon a lull when I could interview him. Between car crashes, cocaine-induced suicide attempts , babies being born – not to mention screaming sirens and 100 mph wild road runs – I was too frazzled when the lull finally arrived. But Charlie, ever composed, explained the depth of his commitment in a few simple words. "You want to know why I do all this, Peggy? Well, in Vietnam I killed a lot of people. People I didn't even know. This is to pay back. Makes me feel a lot better."

6. PASSAGE

A discussion of death, from youth through old age, as seen in mountain happenings where the victim either fatally misjudges or willingly embraces the power of the mountains.

In the dense silence that surrounded us, I knelt beside a body that had lain face down for seven months, six of them frozen, at 13,700-foot elevation. We gently turned him over while I held my breath. I glanced first at his face and couldn't move my eyes away. The scalp and hair remained but maggots had consumed the face and a masterful sculpture of chalk-white marble was left, a chiseled bone structure so fine and strong in its sloping planes and angular ridges that I saw the victim himself and murmured, "What a handsome man." He gazed directly at me; his jaws, with their fine teeth, relaxed in a smile. I was meeting death again, coming to terms in my own mind with the phenomenon that nobody discusses, that fills people with terror, and that waits for us all.

The month was August of my third summer in rescue work. The previous day a hiker, an 18-year-old chap from London, visiting Colorado for some mountain hiking, was traversing the tortured face of 14,238-foot Mount Cameron in the Mosquito Range northeast of Leadville. He had stumbled upon the single-engine plane wreckage on a rock slide hidden between two jagged ribs. He was stunned to see a clawlike hand rising out of the debris – a debris so crushed that he took the wreckage to be a helicopter. From a victim's trouser pocket he removed a checkbook and the aircraft registration, and climbed down the mountain to report his find to the sheriff. I was one of 22 members from several Colorado rescue groups and the Civil Air Patrol who gathered to make the difficult and dangerous body recoveries.

The previous December the same single-engine aircraft had been en route to Salt Lake for a funeral, when the plane vanished from Denver radar near Fairplay. Aboard were Larry, the pilot (a retired Air Force major general), his brother Danny and Danny's wife Janet. Larry hadn't filed a flight plan, and the emergency locator transmitter in the tail of the aircraft was silent.

The following day, during the search for the missing plane, I had pressed my forehead for two hours against the cold window of a Chinook, looking for signs of a crash. The general's plane had disappeared during a heavy snowfall. In our slow, detailed – and too close to the ground – searching back and forth over a bleak and barren upland, I felt that only the warm engine would project above the white blanket spread below us. We spent four hours in the air – two hours were taken up by getting there and back – leaving the usual limit of two hours for searching in the forbidding weather. Perhaps it was a token search for a vague site in a vast alpine land. Regardless, we were unsuccessful.

Seven months of silence had passed before the hiker made his shocking discovery, and that silence continued now while teams moved in slow motion under a piercing sun. Rescue volunteers from Alpine, Summit, Vail, Chaffee, Larimer and El Paso teams had driven four-wheel-drive trucks up Mount Bross, the neighboring mountain, on an untamed mining road, and parked on the saddle it shared with Cameron. When the first team located the crash site from the hiker's description and a helicopter fly-over, they found two bodies in the cockpit and one thrown clear. I came with the second team, and we gingerly crossed loose and skiddish rocks for the half mile to the site on the face.

Looking at the body of the man thrown clear, my emotions reeled. Yet this body recovery wasn't my first. Without thinking of the months that allowed for decomposition, I had assumed that the passengers would resemble those in an earlier body recovery, which had taken place only three days after impact. How far off I was. Glancing around at the 20 men – and a young woman on her first mission – I sensed the strength of their feelings, held down by a steel fist. Only their blank eyes gave them away.

I tugged surgical gloves over my hands and tied a large handkerchief across my nose to keep out the stench. From the trousers of the ejected victim, a Civil Air Patrol member snipped off the back pocket containing the wallet, lifted the ring from his withered and black, clawed finger, and cut belt loops to release the belt buckle; he placed them in a bag to be enclosed with the body. I printed "Danny K" on a hospital bracelet and wrapped it around his dried, rigid wrist. I knew exactly where I was, and what I was doing. However, my sensitivities were exploding within.

Aware of the teeming maggots in his abdomen, three of us gingerly lifted the body, laid it on a black body bag, and zipped it closed. The condition of the corpse was such that I wondered how the mortician could steady himself. The bag was heavily perfumed, and the strong, rich fragrance masked the disagreeable odor.

A sturdy Stokes litter, made of tubular steel and weighing 25 pounds, was brought alongside and we placed the body bag in it, using nylon webbing, woven back and forth across the litter top, to securely lace him down. The lower end of a nylon climbing rope was attached to the litter, the upper end to a brake system from which four of us and the litter would hang. I removed the surgical gloves and handkerchief, and bent over to take hold of my corner of the litter.

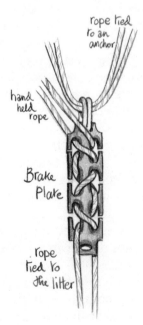

rope tied to an anchor

hand held rope

Brake Plate

rope tied to the litter

As litter captain I was to give commands: "Anyone not ready?" "Loading the litter" (to prepare the brakeman). "Lift on three." "Down slow." But I couldn't speak. I was numb and overwhelmed. Ashes to ashes, dust to dust. We lifted the litter, descending past the crumbled fuselage still clinging tenaciously to the mountain. I glanced at the bodies of the pilot and the woman lying inside and was relieved to start down the 1,500-foot face; I had already seen all my emotions could handle.

I worried about my strong reaction to the wife – this was the first time I had taken part in a rescue effort involving a dead woman. Perhaps due to lack of sleep, or to the high elevation and its greatly reduced oxygen, or to the fact that I too was a woman, I feared a flood of tears. The men who train us say we are to be professional and impersonal. But what would a woman trainer say? I asked myself. In years since, my arms have supported crumbling women – and an occasional man – when my instincts told me to do so.

Our route to the bottom of Cameron's face was on an abrupt and loose rock slide, where we were exposed to the sudden tumbling of more rocks from the flaking walls threatening on either side. But I didn't see the danger. Even when I realized two of our litter bearers were novices and lost their balance, causing all four of us to collapse onto the sharp rock edges, I accepted it stoically. One brakeman, new and untrained in rescue work, erred by letting the rope start through the brake when he saw we were on our feet but before he heard our command; because we stood on unsteady feet, we immediately fell back down. Despite these practical problems, my mind was preoccupied. I was lost to reality. I wanted to stop the litter and give time to my thoughts, but we had to move along. Two litters, each containing a victim, were to follow, and we were to set up more brake systems as we dropped down the face.

I was stretched to the limit. To remain in that condition for hours means one doesn't snap back quickly. However, after the bodies were in the sheriff's four-wheel-drive, rescuers stood on the flower-strewn meadow and milled around, talking, laughing, renewing friendships from previous missions. They were letting go and ignoring the three waiting in their litters. One can of beer was shared. Brandon Bennett, an El Paso member, walked a hundred yards away to be quiet and to calm himself. He had come on the mission directly from his night shift as a sheriff's deputy, going 36 hours without sleep. I found a stream and splashed my fatigue away.

A litter team of three men and Peggy rests while lowering a body down a   mountain.

The pilot and his passengers had lain under sunshine and snow, unknown until the Londoner's discovery. From Kite Lake, a small body of water at treeline, the crash site appeared to be a pile of rocks. We knew it was invisible from side slopes and summit, on a face too dangerous to traverse on foot. The illusion of the wreckage echoed the other crude heaps of loose, jagged rocks that clutched the precariously pitched wall. An emergency signal hadn't been picked up; judging by the intensity of the impact on the massive cliffs of Cameron – metal from the aircraft intruded into cracks in the rock wall – a transmitter could have been destroyed.

Larry, commander of a fighter wing for two years in Vietnam and Thailand, had almost 5,000 hours in F-4s. He was reportedly a "very, very experienced pilot." Perhaps also too confident. He took off at 2:15 in the afternoon, too late in the day; early arrival of the winter night can surprise the unaware. Colorado pilots don't fly over the Rockies at night. They are "out," or on the ground, by nightfall at the latest. Is that long puff of white a cloud or a snowfield? Both hide granite, unyielding granite. The rule obeyed by light aircraft is: All mountain flights are on the ground by noon. Like the climber's rule for lightning storms: Everybody off the summit by noon.

Larry failed to file a flight plan. Nobody knew his route, although Denver radar fixed him near Fairplay – but just where near Fairplay? He chose his own direct route between Denver and Salt Lake, "above it all," ignoring safer routes. In the mountains pilots are supposed to fly over a route suggested on the sectional aeronautical charts. These carefully designed routes avoid the storm-tossed peaks – peaks that soared along Larry's route from 14,000 to 14,433 feet, as well as an endless supply of 13,000- and 12,000-foot summits.

Storms – his weather report predicted one – produce winds that are forced upwards by a mountain slope, giving an updraft that can carry a plane into the clouds for a heavy coat of ice. If instruments ice up or if the pilot can't believe the astounding information they're relaying, the flight can become very hazardous. Storms cause down-drafts with remarkable strength, and these can quickly drop a low-flying light plane out of control to the ground. Also, a storm's headwinds, if severe, cancel much of the speed of an aircraft cruising with only 150 horsepower. Most storms around the high Rockies have snowfall – more accurately, blinding blizzards – and they can occur in December or in July. But winds don't really need a storm; they can roar effectively all on their own.

To me, mountain flying in a single-engine aircraft is too horrible to contemplate. During a discussion with Saundra Stienmier, a long-time pilot and the wife of our physician member, Dick, on the dangers of mountain flying, she offered me a ride.

"Oh, no! I'd never go up in a small plane."

"Why not?" She argued. "It's safer than driving your truck."

"No way!" I explained. "I've worked too many aircraft crashes."

After the body recoveries, a long drive through the mountains brought us to our homes late that night, yet I was up early to walk through my flower garden and absorb the rich color and optimism of the daylilies and delphinium in the morning light. These flowers stablized my vivid emotions, their brilliant profusion of petals swept away the raw shock that caused me to see my family and home life as strangers, only death as a real existence. To be effective I had to switch gears; my husband, four grown children and the daily ritual must be cemented into a foundation which could not crumble in the face of these spiritual gropings. I would experience this powerful reaction to death again and again. Body recoveries occur year after year; with each one I more clearly realize the fragile veil between life and death.

Woods Rose

My compassion isn't always directed to the victim. Sometimes I observe the family member or reporting party and recognize the inner stress that builds steadily without release, a dam waiting to overflow. When we conduct a search or a rescue, and the family is not visible, we are nevertheless keenly aware of their existence. On unpleasant and hazardous body recoveries, like the one on Mount Cameron, I sustain myself by muttering, "This is awful, but think of the family – " a family I rarely meet and from whom I can hardly expect a "thank you."

When family members are present at mission base, their behavior is unpredictable. During the rescue briefing for a crashed aircraft on Mount Taylor, two ranchers stood aside, their faces somber and voices silent. Realizing they were family representatives, and feeling embarrassment over our loud discussions and bursts of laughter, I walked over to apologize. "We are so intent on our rescue that we sometimes forget the family is here." Their eyes fixed on mine. There was a tentative nod of understanding, then the masks of mourning returned and I wandered away.

Sometimes family members arrive wearing expressions of acceptance, as though they already know the consequences. I remember one early winter, watching a pickup drive into Leadville's airport – at 10,000 feet, the highest in the country. The driver, his face tooled leather from many years in the Colorado sun, pulled his vehicle close to the runway, where he could face the occasional private plane that landed. He was waiting for his 22-year-old son – a passenger, along with a doctor, a businessman and a lawyer who was the pilot of the small private plane that was two days overdue. They had been flying from Wyoming to their homes in southern Colorado. I gently asked this father, "Where are the other three families?"

He replied quietly, "I phone them every day with any news. My wife's a Christian and she stayed home to help the wives. You see, they're not Christians."

While the Chinook pilots rested in the airport from their precise flying up over 14,000 feet along the snow-packed gorges and over the windblown ridges, I said to the father, "Come, sit with our team out in the warm sunshine." He wasn't a large man, but there was considerable strength in his unwavering eyes. I admired his simple dignity and sensed his familiarity with death.

"They got a fine boy there," the father murmured about his son, gazing beyond the runway to the guilty peaks white with autumn snow.

In Denver, late the day before, the pilot had refueled the plane and, in defiance of a storm ahead, started over the mountains. Recently licensed, he wasn't rated for instrument flying. They overloaded the plane with a large dog and 37 frozen pheasants. A blizzard added heavy ice to the wings. The pilot chose a direct route over the shoulders of Colorado's great peaks, a dozen of them over 14,000 feet. The recommended route on the charts is south from Denver, over the plains to Walsenburg, then west across Cumbres Pass to Cortez; the aircraft is then always over roads, valleys, people and emergency-landing choices. Some downed aircraft are still missing because nobody can find them in the wilderness. The pilot, disoriented from lack of visibility in the heavy snowfall and extreme turbulence in the strong winds, as well as instrument readings he didn't believe, radioed a frantic call, "Mayday! Mayday!" A jetliner flying above the weather responded and alerted Denver radar, which attempted to lead the lost pilot to the runway lights of the Leadville airport. "I'm making a thirty-degree turn," he reported – and wasn't heard from again.

We were anxious to find survivors, but the emergency locator transmitter wasn't activated. Maybe it had been damaged in the crash, or someone had previously removed it, or the batteries were stale. We had no other way to trace the plane, which could be obscured by snow on the unforgiving peaks that stretch into the sky, or among conifers in the deep valleys. The Chinook pilots flew close to the snow-packed couloirs (almost vertical gorges high on the mountainside) while we studied every bump that projected through the snowcrust. Tom, a Denver engineer, peered into an infrared sensor while sitting in the icy rotor wind blowing though the helicopter's open door. He found some suspicious rocks, but when the pilots swung close, we saw they weren't a warm aircraft engine. At the end of the week the search teams departed, and the stoic father drove slowly home without his son. The next summer Civil Air Patrol members on a training exercise spotted four bodies and the scattered wreckage of the Cessna 182 Skylane below treeline on 12,700-foot Chicago Ridge, north of our search area.

During most searches a family member or reporting party walks aimlessly about base camp, like the father in the above search, his anxiety level growing higher by the hour as searchers try to shield him from unsettling radio reports coming from teams. We tie orange surveyor's ribbon around his arm in an attempt to isolate

orange flagging

him, and as a warning to members to watch their statements. We say to him, "Now we can find you when you are needed."

But isolation is not always possible. On a summer mission to Mount Aeolus in the Needle Mountains of the San Juan Range north of Durango – our second search there in my three years with the team – I was alone with Marshall, the reporting party, and unable to shield him from the radio messages. His close friend, Paul, a young computer programmer, had failed to return after trying for the 14,183-foot summit. Marshall had turned back earlier at 12,500 feet.

Both men were visiting from Del Mar, California, and were seasoned hikers, not experienced climbers. To reach these inspiring but treacherous peaks ringing Chicago Basin, the two rode the Durango & Silverton Narrow Gauge Railroad to a drop-off point and hiked eight hours up the trail to the peaks.

Paul wore jogging shoes for a fourteener that is hardly known as a walk-up. He left his pack on a ridge – he had no food, water or warm clothing, much less shelter. When Marshall, nervous on the abruptly pitched smooth slabs, turned back, Paul continued alone. Paul didn't know of the preferred summit route on the east side.

On the second morning, search teams made up from Larimer, Alpine, San Juan, La Plata, Western State and El Paso blanketed the mountain. I beckoned to Marshall, "C'mon along and be the eighth on my team. We're climbing to search the cliffs on the west side." I noted the sudden interest in his eyes as he moved ahead of me with exquisite balance.

When we reached 13,000 feet, a message from an El Paso team on the east knife-edge ridge came over my radio: "We've a possible sighting of a body." I panicked. I was alone beside Marshall, with my team, made up of several search groups, scattered in a line across the mountainside. This dilemma had not occurred to me when I asked him to join me. Marshall would have to face the facts as they unfolded.

"You realize," I suggested softly, "that Paul may be injured, unconscious or gone." I couldn't utter the word "dead," yet that was what I expected. Yes, he knew. I became highly nervous and blurted out, "This isn't the way we do it. You shouldn't be up here. I only brought you because you were going crazy in base. You're not to hear these radio messages. Some are in code to hide information from you. Can you handle this?"

He replied soberly, "You couldn't tear me away from the radio."

We continued to climb up over sloping rock cliffs in silence. Marshall was quiet and withdrawn.

My adrenaline level rose alarmingly when the radio brought, "It's a body. The Alpine team will go. They're closest."

While sitting anxiously in lush grass above a cliff, Ed, an El Paso member, and I each wrapped an arm around Marshall. I looked across at Sunlight and Windom, two other 14,000-foot peaks hanging over the valley, but didn't see them. Soon the radio transmitted the message, "I have Charlie and he isn't feeling too good."

I forced myself to face Marshall and say, "Charlie is code for Paul if he's found dead." He slumped in our arms, and I heard myself whisper, "I'm sorry, Marshall, damned sorry." All the routes to the summit are dangerous, especially the thin rock ridge he traversed, and from which he tumbled in a 500-foot free-fall.

We slowly descended the slippery grass to base, where a tanned Colorado mounted ranger, wearing cowboy boots, wide-brimmed hat and chaps, stood close in front of me and in a concerned voice asked, "How'd you deal with it up there?" I repeated my words to Marshall, and it all came back: the tension, my restrained thoughts, the tragedy of the death. The stress drained out of me in tears that ran unwiped down my face.

More tears flooded a month later when I was in California near Paul's parents and contacted them by phone. When I identified myself to the mother, her voice immediately broke into wrenching sobs, and I forgot my vow to be professional. Her first words were, "Did he suffer?" I answered truthfully: "No. One moment he was breathing; the next moment he wasn't." We cried, and I listened while she talked of her son.

Rescuers in a fatality don't always cry. After a mission, boisterous play among members releases the gut-deep emotion that socks us into silence when we lift a warm, limp body into a black body bag and zipper it out of sight. If the victim is close in age to the rescuer, or to the child of a rescuer, the impact is devastating.

I recall the handsome and perfect body of Jeffrey, a 17-year-old lad, who, scrambling in smooth-soled shoes with two high school friends, had slipped to his death down the polished rocks of Rosa Cascades on the Pikes Peak massif. After I climbed the slippery scree and the slanting, wet rocks of the lower cascades and saw his body, clad only in shorts and socks, lying on his back across a ledge beside the waterfall, I retreated into deep despair. I wanted to say, "He'll come back to life any minute, just wait, he's not dead forever. It can't be, please wait!" But the two ambulance paramedics had a look of surrender, so I remained quiet.

The scene around the fallen youth was hushed, faces grim. When a command was given, the voice was low and barely audible. Skee told Kevin to take over the litter, while he would climb higher and set up a brake system. I watched Kevin – tall, straw-haired and only four years older than Jeffrey – stand aside as if in a fog, saying nothing, his face expressionless. Later, he would tell me he was shattered. Pulling himself together, Kevin turned to me. "Get the two litter halves together and attach the rope." I forgot to remove the two pack frames that carry the litter halves, and had to be reminded. I started to tie the rope to the foot of the litter instead of to the head before I caught myself. I made the tail of the bowline knot too long. Kevin had nothing on my fog. After almost four years of rescues I knew the techniques perfectly – but somehow, the presence of the young man lying at my feet stupefied me.

I was one of the four litter bearers for the first two brake systems, each almost 200 feet long, that dropped down vertical rock ledges, over scratchy thimbleberry and stiff mountain mahogany, on a narrow trail covered with scree pebbles that ran along a hillside tilted sideways. Commands and complaints were grunted; the route was tough. Then the steepness lessened and the half-mile carry became easier. Talking, teasing and joking began, laughter followed. The litter, now clamped over an airplane tire, brought running and exuberance, a wild release of suppressed stress when we briefly forgot the victim among us. We burst onto the trailhead, raucous, panting, tired, to face two grim morticians, the shocked press and rolling TV cameras.

"You fellows have to stop the fooling around." The television technician growled. "We can hear one of your people laughing on the audio."

During the following nights, and even the days, shafts of sadness for the mother and for the lad's brief life, shot through my mind. I felt a powerful empathy with the mother, who hadn't wanted Jeffrey to go, for fear of an accident, and whose son was the age of our youngest daughter. Surely a rescuer is divided in half – the subdued, the compassionate, contrasted with the untamed, the uninhibited.

Our participation in that body recovery lasted only two hours; sometimes a search lasts three, four or even five days, and if the lost person hasn't been found, then it's the coordinator's difficult job to inform the family the search is being closed. Emergency vehicles, the communication trailer, searchers' cars, the helicopter and the press cars are taken away, and the mountain is silent once again. The body of the victim doesn't go away. It absorbs the heat of the sun as the day slowly slips by; it lies under the stars of the lonely night.

The body attracts scavengers from the sky: the vulture, raven, crow, magpie and fly, who start cleansing the dead matter from the mountain. The bear, raccoon, weasel, fox, coyote, porcupine and mice appear and carry body parts for considerable distances, scattering the bones through the forest. They may not be scattered

a raven

far, but they are never as I had once envisioned: the exact pattern of a skeleton, skull to toe, lying on the ground.

The skull is heavy and usually found close to the final rest-ing place. The Texas pilot, who walked away from the air crash on Mount Yale for help and froze to death a half mile away was identified nine months later by comparing his den-tal charts with a skull lying close to where he stopped. His clothes also remained, but small animals had shredded them and taken wisps of material to line their nests. A companion and I picked up his shoulder blade 18 months later about 100 yards from where he halted; some of his other bones were never located.

Finally nothing remains; the fungus, mite, earthworm and bacteria in the soil have joined to break down and free the basic chemicals for use by live organisms. The body hasn't dis-appeared; rather, it has blended into the earth.

The scavengers aren't hesitant about their function in life. When a plane crashed on Williams Pass south of Mount Princeton in the Sawatch Range, in my second summer of res-cue work, I was camped over the ridge. I watched the Civil Air Patrol fly, searching for a wreckage. The pilot of the downed aircraft, flying from his sea-level home in Southern California, carried three passengers bound for a light-aircraft convention in Illinois. He didn't file a flight plan. The route he chose is guarded by three peaks well over 14,000 and rec-ommended for high-performance aircraft, which his was not.

A family in a campground on the western slope watched the pilot enter a box canyon at a low altitude. When he didn't fly back out, they reported the incident to the sheriff. The pilot intended to fly north out of the box canyon, and cross 11,766-foot Williams Pass. He just barely cleared the canyon wall, when his heart must have stopped to see the pass, a mile ahead and 400 feet above his aircraft. The warm midday air and the high elevation caused a low air density – his horse-power lessened, his propeller efficiency dropped. Despite full throttle, he began to shear spruce tops. Then trunks of spruce trees. Until he cartwheeled to the ground at 11,600. The emer-gency transmitter didn't function, and without a flight plan he wasn't overdue. Three days later convention friends in-quired after him, and a search was launched. The Civil Air Pa-trol had heard about the low-flying plane and taken to the air. However, two more days elapsed before the scattered debris was sighted in the spruce on Williams Pass. In that brief time animals had ravaged the bodies of the four occupants.

To a hiker moving along a forest trail or climbing above treeline, the countryside seems quiet and without any animal life. Sit silently on the ground for a while and all the occupants emerge. Birds fly in and out of every tree hole, marmots tumble with each other across the meadow, and pikas continue gathering their winter hay stack. When the sun sets, a coyote may chase a tired deer across the other side of the meadow, or a raccoon will stare at you, while a porcupine sits on a tree branch at night. The bear is there but you see only his prints. The place is a madhouse of activity, and the sanitation crew is ever present.

These animals reduce the carrion in the forest, yet are not numerous compared to the maggots that clean a skeleton with speed and perfection. A maggot is a legless and soft-bodied baby fly; a larva, most often without eyes or even a head. When mature, the female astutely lays her eggs, which hatch in a few days, on a food source. Such facts of nature can solve mysteries, as in this example involving an autumn search for a man from Minnesota.

When Scott, a young diabetic doctor, arrived in October near Wolf Creek Pass, north of Pagosa Springs in the San Juan Range, to hunt elk with bow and arrow, he brought a supply of insulin. At dawn the first morning, he and his companion agreed to go their separate ways and return to camp by mid-morning. Scott was a "sit" hunter – one who sits along an elk trail, waiting for the elk to walk by – in contrast to a "stalk" hunter, who tracks. With his camouflage clothing and blackened face, elk wouldn't see Scott. Neither would searchers. The doctor failed to appear by late afternoon. His friend radioed him missing and a search was launched.

After an unsuccessful two days with local teams, the sheriff called the state coordinator for assistance on the third day, and Daniel Lockhart and I from El Paso County, as well as members of five other teams, were picked up by an Air Force C-130 early the fourth day. The field leader stood by the radio tent on the edge of a grassy meadow and briefed us. "This man can handle stress, is in good shape, and has done considerable camping. He took two vials of insulin, a syringe and a few candy bars with him. He's got a compass, but no map, so is probably lost."

Late the next afternoon search dogs and their handlers, inserted by helicopter and working into the breeze, picked up the scent which led to the doctor's body lying face down in the shallow water of a drainage ravine three miles from base. Scott's death was a shock to all the searchers. The deputy coroner told us, "Death occurred the first night the doctor was lost out here." We were mystified by his statement until the autopsy report revealed that fly (Diptera) eggs were found on his hair and maggots on his shoulder. The time required for the eggs to hatch dated his death.

The time and cause of death in mountain missions is usually an educated guess. Experienced and trained personnel put together the weather, mental and physical condition of victim, terrain, location and distance from last-seen point. To these factors is added an exhaustive autopsy. A probable cause of death results. As a Mineral County official commented, "Only the victim really knows what happened, and he ain't tellin'."

The coroner had proven the doctor's day of death but not the cause of it. We believed that Scott's irrational behavior – half-hearted and unsuccessful fire attempts, glasses broken and vest on ground, gloves unworn and inside-out, insulin vials and syringe missing, bow and quiver containing arrows all missing, and body facedown in shallow water – indicated probable hypothermia. I puzzled over the possibilities until summer, when a law-enforcement officer said to me, "Scott didn't carry any insulin on his morning elk hunt, Peggy. Then he got lost and that night went into a fatal diabetic coma."

"But our briefing clearly said he took insulin with him that morning."

"Well, he didn't. When his family found out an Army Chinook isn't permitted to search for a dead person, they felt that volunteer searchers wouldn't come either, so in their desperation to recover his body, they decided to pretend he had had an insulin supply with him." The missing insulin and map brought down Scott's life.

Other deaths occur on purpose, planned and embraced, because of what appears to them at the time to be insurmountable difficulties. I used to be upset when responding to a suicide. What a tragic waste of life! That thought was chased away after two years in rescue work, to be replaced by humility and understanding, as the following briefing proceeded.

"Our victim, Duane, is married, thirty-two years old," explained the deputy. "He left a suicide note to his wife: Take care of the kids. You are stronger than I am, this is the easy way out . . ." A motorcycle accident five years before had left Duane with a plate in his skull, hearing aids and medication for seizures. Now he was missing.

Battle Mountain, near Vail in the Gore Range, where his truck was found, is covered with aspen-fringed meadows and dense drifts of spruce – we'd never find him in all that foliage. But during our sweeps in the helicopter just above tree level, a rocky projection appeared before the pilots. On it lay his T-shirt and blue jacket, glasses and hearing aids, cigarettes and lighter. We knew he'd be somewhere below on the thick grass that grew around the aspen trunks. Duane had chosen a high promontory, and we are taught that suicidal persons typically choose an overlook.

His body, lying under a log, was 600 feet below the rocky point, but death had not been from the jump; his voluntary lack of medication had caused a fatal seizure. "I can't go on with medications that control my life, with machines in my ears to hear people," he wrote in his note to his wife.

Some people are drawn to the mountains out of a misery so pervasive it demands escape, out of an intuitive desire to return to the earth. I learned this only weeks after joining the team. A car, parked for a month on a lonely mountain road 20 miles north of Woodland Park, in the Rampart Range, was registered to Angelina, a beautiful, young prostitute from Denver. The State Patrol told us, "On the seat inside we found a suicide note and will, the receipt for a .22-caliber pistol, and a box of ammunition with five bullets missing."

I had studied search techniques in books and had listened avidly at a training session on the subject. Now here was my first search; however, I felt cynical over her disappearance. Surely Angelina had set the stage for an apparent suicide, and now was far away. In our briefing we had learned she was under protective custody as a witness for the Federal Bureau of Investigation.

Our team probed in a loose and long line through the thin ponderosa forest, checking snow patches and mud for footprints. We didn't call her name and listen – she was alive and away from the scene, or dead and unable to hear our voices. We peered among the thick chokecherries and wild

junipers growing below the nearby precipices and hiked for
hours over the gently sloping, wooded hills.

The next day a search dog discovered her body deep in a
rock crevice, an earthly womb, into which she had crawled to
depart from her overwhelming problems. The dog handler
told me, "She was invisible to you, but my dog had no problem finding her body."

Sometimes I wonder about the thin line between suicide
and apathy, particularly in older people like Amy, a lost 81-
year-old resident of Cañon City. Nine months after our search
for her was canceled, a wrangler returned to the stable at the
Royal Gorge Park, that borders the Arkansas River west of
Cañon City, and blurted out, "I seen a skull in the middle of
that abandoned horse trail. About fifteen feet farther on down
the trail are some leg bones and a backbone with ribs, then farther are arm and hand bones inside sleeves!" The remains
were identified as Amy.

One afternoon in October, Amy had come home to discover a cleaning crew in her apartment, and it was apparently
the final irritation. The courts had appointed a guardian who
had taken away her control and given her an allowance. Amy
had been giving away large amounts of money and the guardian felt she was showing signs of senility. Angry after dis-
covering the cleaning crew, the harassed woman stormed
down to the bank and told them of her displeasure; then she
set off on foot for the Royal Gorge, seven miles west of town,
where the gathering darkness brought a penetrating chill.
Never seen or heard from again, searchers believed Amy had
died somewhere among the spreading piñon pines. The
weary woman must have grown weak, stumbled and collapsed on the trail in the still darkness, and perhaps looked
up at the cold stars until she fell asleep. If so, then death came
with her consent in peaceful surroundings.

For me, to become part of the wilderness, open and free, is
preferable to being cooped up in a hospital bed, or worse still,
a box in the ground. To have one's ashes cast along a limpid
stream on a mountainside, open to the sky, to lie under the
snowfall, to nourish rock primrose and saxafrage, to feel the
warmth of the spring melt – those are for the spirit to look forward to after death.

Glacier Lily

Peggy snowshoes down an alpine slope to the crashed Huey.

7. HUNTERS ARE HUNTED

Spring brings violent downdrafts over the Continental Divide. A single-engine plane, attempting to pierce the winds, disappears. Its rescuer, a helicopter, is missing.

 The little Huey helicopter lay ruptured in spring snow, like a bird that had swooped down in a swift attack on its prey only to collide with the earth. The top rotor was bent over, its long blades twisted – feathers in disarray. But the illusion ceased when I glanced at three passengers in Army green standing alongside. Flying close overhead in a Chinook, I looked at our commander, Captain Ron, who was beside me hanging out the open door, and pulled off my mitten to expose three fingers. He stretched five gloved fingers in reply. Where were the other two soldiers? In the bird?

The night before, during Easter week, a page had asked us to fly at dawn to seek two downed aircraft near Monarch Pass, but no details were offered. Strange, having two down at once in the same mountain terrain. Monarch Pass, at 11,300 feet and 23 miles west of Salida, is on the Continental Divide, in the Sawatch Range; it separates the headwaters of the South Arkansas River that flows east from waters that flow west to the Colorado River.

Before daylight nine of us hurried through empty streets to await the Chinook on the frozen grass at Fort Carson. Nobody talked. A distraction could mean a backpack left behind in a car trunk, or a litter forgotten on the field.

I trembled to watch the sinister insect slowly approach at daybreak, its landing lights staring at us. Hard to believe people were inside. We stomped up the ramp and dropped our gear down the center of the metal floor, where a crewman lashed it securely with webbing. I sat on the red canvas bench that drops along from the fuselage wall, a seat belt tightly drawn over my hips, and tried to appear confident on my second Chinook mission after only six months in rescue work. Mel, our field leader, took a seat and shouted through my ear plugs, "Yesterday a Huey flew near Monarch Pass searching for a missing plane. Now the Huey's missing!" I didn't care where we flew – just to be aboard was enough. I love the fuel smell, the strong vibrations from two rotors and the Army crew dressed in flight suits topped by helmets fit for outer space.

Approaching the Salida airport, after an hour's flight time, Captain Ron heard by aircraft radio from a Denver Channel 9 helicopter piloted by Jug Hill: "We've got the Huey in sight. It's on the side of Cyclone Mountain."

"We won't check in with the Civil Air Patrol at airport base," Captain Ron radioed back. "We're flying straight over." The Army goes straightaway for its own men. The Civil Air Patrol wasn't happy with the snub.

After passing above Salida, the aircraft took a course west for 13,657-foot Cyclone Mountain, one of the birthplaces of the South Arkansas River. Actually I had no idea of our location. Passengers in a Chinook are always confused. Looking through the few circular helicopter windows while in flight must be the same frustration a baby bird endures in his tree-hole nest. Even if the waters of the South Arkansas's North Fork, flowing between peaks over 13,000, were visible on this early March flight, the layer upon layer of snow from strong winter storms would have concealed the stream from us. However, when I glimpsed white in the window across the fuselage – and it wasn't clouds – and when I felt the Chinook being shaken in the mouth of the wind, then I knew Cyclone was nearby.

Suddenly the rotors changed pitch. Captain Ron left the commander's seat behind the pilots, walked to the side door and threw open its upper half. Could be the Huey crash site. Afraid of missing something, I unbuckled, moved to the bench next to Ron and rebuckled. My face stiffened from blasts of frigid air driven in by the rotors. No snow was falling from the somber sky, but wind blew ground-snow into clouds that swirled above our ship. Two soldiers of the five reportedly on the flight weren't visible in the depressing scene below. Evidently we had no radio contact with the Huey crew, because Captain Ron was tense about the missing two.

He slammed the door, and we belted for landing. A Chinook comes straight down, drops its rear to the earth, then hesitates before lowering the front – a more eccentric manner of landing I've never seen in other aircraft or flying birds. When ground-snow in the wind joined snow from the rotor blast, our windows turned white and we knew the back end was on the ground. But only for a second. A severe gust tilted the chopper, and we soared into the air. Moving higher onto a white plateau, the pilots dropped for another landing, but again the wind wrapped its brawn around the Chinook. A third attempt higher up aborted. A fourth was successful.

My stomach had shrunken to minimal size, when the gale vanished briefly and, with the crew chief's signal, we leaped up, grabbed our packs and raced out the ramp, dropping on deep snow in a high, flat basin of Cyclone.

"Without the weight of the ship," the co-pilot told me later, "we never could have withstood those sixty-mile-an-hour winds and held her down in a landing." (To a helicopter pilot, "landing" means hovering up to eight feet over the snow surface, just close enough for passengers to jump from the ramp.)

Rotors twirled madly for the Chinook's hover over the snow surface. Ice crystals peppered my face. Leaving my pack with other gear, I ran back to enter the ramp. But the aircraft was gone, climbing in a steep bank through mists to low snow clouds.

"Damn, you took off with my snowshoes!" I shouted toward the pilots. But wind chased my words away.

"Peggy, relax, I carried out two pairs," a member offered.

Others also had left gear in the Chinook – consolation for me.

Standing among us, dressed in winter khaki, was a soldier from our Chinook. Captain Ron glared at him and demanded, "What in hell are you doing here?"

"Sir, I won't give you any trouble, I promise you." Told not to leave the aircraft, he had done so nevertheless, taking a camera for crash-site photos but no heavy clothing, sleeping bag, food or water. If the chopper couldn't return, he would probably freeze in silence rather than admit his mistake.

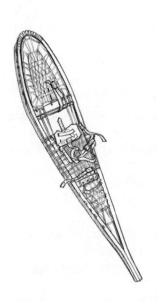

A few of the group quickly strapped on snowshoes and left for the Huey; others remained to fiddle with snowshoe bindings. When mine were on, I stood up and peered through my goggles across a barren snowfield, etched only by the shadow of a winding snowshoe track. The isolation beckoned me to follow solo.

Before the snowfield began, sharp rocky ledges protruded high above the snow; I unstrapped my snowshoes so I could climb down over them. Gale winds were increasing alarmingly as I slowly made my way forward. When a refuge was needed, I closed my eyes and hugged a sturdy rock – if I got blown off, the rock was coming with me.

After the cliff, I saw soft, gently sloping fields of blinding white that flowed downhill to disappear under dark fingers of spruce reaching up from the valley to high-country cold. This ragged treeline below told me our elevation was well over 12,000 feet, but we seemed even higher. The squall, filled with vitality and strength, was shoving clouds against lofty summits just short of 14,000 feet. Clouds broke or shredded into mists, and I saw peaks, their black ribs and ridges heavily draped with snow, hanging in space encircled by ethereal clouds. "My God, I must be in Heaven!" I gasped out loud. When gusts became too strong on the snowfield, I stood sideways and bent over, braced against the force, until the air quieted. My face was buried in ice crystals. For one moment during the half-mile trek, the cloud-cover thinned over my head, and I briefly felt the warmth of a spring sun on my cheeks.

From my solitude and joy in the majestic scene, an emotional high was building, until I snowshoed over a lip and saw the Huey, a UH-lV Bell Helicopter, embedded in snow, never to fly again. Far below, our primitive-looking Chinook sat over wind-packed crusts, wheels buried, rotor blades hanging limp above silent motors. While 15 tons of Chinook slowly sank into five feet of snow, hidden rocks punched gaping holes into the metal plates of the fuselage – only this wouldn't be discovered until days later at Fort Carson.

"Why didn't you answer my calls, Peggy?" Mel asked when I reached the wreckage.

"Oh, I forgot you gave me a radio. Didn't turn it on." I knew he understood the emotions that carried me from reality, but with soldiers listening, I said no more.

"Well, you're one of the litter bearers," Mel shouted through the wind. Litter bearers? So then, the two missing soldiers were injured and had been lying in the crashed aircraft.

The two litter halves were joined, and the injured co-pilot was helped from the Huey. Despite two compressed vertabrae, he looked at the ground blizzard raging, then at the four litter bearers, and decided he could walk the quarter mile to the Chinook below. What a relief! I had been wondering how I would manage the trek with five-foot snow-

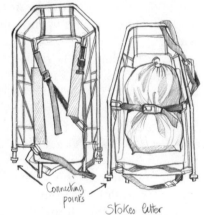

Connecting points

Stokes Litter

shoes strapped on my boots. Carrying rescue gear, we joined the limping and battered crew on a slow shuffle over an icy crust to our helicopter. Since soldiers look alike in a blizzard, I never identified the other injured one.

Too many pilots laugh at the slow and clumsy Chinook. But as he entered the door, uninjured, this Huey pilot, 43-year-old Chief Warrant Officer Frank Rush, said, "I'll never bad-mouth a Chinook again." A Wyoming native, he had had more than 6,000 hours flying helicopters during two tours in Vietnam.

The Huey crew removed their boots and socks to revive dead-cold feet, numb from the bitter night. I took the foot of the medic, Spec. 4 Steve Johnson, in my warm hands – the foot of a marble statue in wintertime. The night had gone close to zero with a 50-knot wind, giving a chill factor outside the Huey of minus 50 degrees. No wonder their feet had no sensation. Until recent years, freezing extremities were "restored" by rubbing with ice or snow, but rubbing further damages the injured tissues and blood vessels, and the added cold is even worse. Gradual rewarming isn't recommended either, nor are drugs to prevent blood clotting or to dilate blood vessels.

The Huey carried ample water for drinking, but the harsh cold had frozen it. Still, with 200 gallons of fuel on board, nobody lit a fire to melt it. The crew had rations, sleeping bags and long underwear; but those survival items may not be as important as having water to drink. A dehydrated person isn't a happy person – the body is weak, the brain is dizzy, the stomach is nauseated, and cramps strike without notice. Eating snow doesn't provide much water; besides it takes body heat to melt the snow and then to warm the freezing snow-water.

With all that fuel, nobody smoked a cigarette. Anyway, smoking is risky in the winter mountains. Nicotine constricts blood vessels in the skin and the reduced heat invites frostbite. Smoking also decreases the body's ability to carry oxygen. Same caution goes for alcohol; it expands the blood vessels and heat is lost. (The victim dies faster but happier.) People need a full deck around the mountains. City habits are out.

Leaning across the cabin, I asked Lt. Gary Buhler, the injured co-pilot, "Weren't you the co-pilot of the Huey that brought down the Mount Yale survivors?"

"Yes. And I remember talking with you at the hospital," he mumbled with a grin on his stoic face.

Our Chinook pilot on this mission, Chief Warrant Officer J.D. Arnold, had also flown us during the Mount Yale mission. And later I learned that Denver's Channel 9 helicopter, after spotting a smoke grenade from the Huey wreckage, had radioed a private helicopter searching in the air to fly over and mark the location, as the news chopper was low on fuel. The pilot of the private helicopter was the same Chuck – Chuck Demerest – who had taken me with him high up on

Mount Yale. Three pilots from Yale . . . In addition, three heli-copter pilots from Denver television stations, including the late Karen Key, had also been at Mount Yale and now at this Salida mission. Jim Alsum of the Civil Air Patrol and Tom Fiore of Alpine Rescue Team covered both missions. Such a coincidence illustrates how few people in Colorado, whether pilots or team members, are in rescue work.

Departing down Cyclone Gulch, the ship bucked in 60 mph gusts and, in spite of a seat belt, I clung to the bench. I turned to Dick, and shouted, "Scary," in his ear.

"No, only when it goes upside down."

One rescuer, Don Ravenscroft, a powerfully built Air Force Academy officer, turned grey-green. The injured co-pilot dropped his head between his knees to relieve pain from our wild, erratic leaps. I felt fine but had great concern about the "Jesus nuts" which held on the rotors. A Chinook is stressed for moderate turbulence, not the violent tumult we were ex-periencing. When I first rode a Chinook, its blades – three blades to a rotor and two rotors to an aircraft – were of alu-minum alloy. Soon the blades were changed to fiberglass, which has more lift and more flexibility. The ride is the same, the cost is less. I just hoped that the crews had bolted them on tightly. Should the two engines fail, the rotors would autorotate the ship down to a rough landing. If the rotors break off, the bird lands by gravity – in a crash.

"That was the roughest I've ever flown. Wasn't a good place to be flying a bird. Winds were treacherous," the pilot reminisced with me later.

Out of Cyclone Gulch, the pilots headed 30 miles east to make a tight landing in the parking lot of Salida Hospital, al-ready crowded with parked cars and stately trees. Faces filled with amazement crowded the windows. Rotor wash of 125 mph kicked up and sent flying the dust and pebbles of 100 years. The pilots wound down the motors and lowered the ramp.

Captain Ron walked out and was confronted by an indig-nant head nurse in the parking lot. "You're not supposed to land here. You're too big. They're waiting for you at the air-port with two ambulances."

"But we've landed. I'm not going to take off with these injured men." The crew entered the hospital on numb feet, followed by the co-pilot, who crawled on hands and knees.

The day was only half over, and one aircraft rescue was wrapped up. One more to go.

At the Salida airport a kind woman had brought a washtub full of chili and beans for the 40 people milling around in the small terminal. While eating, I asked Mel, "What was a flea-sized Huey doing in high mountains during such weather?"

"Shouldn't have been there. Whoever named Cyclone must have known its wind shears and downdrafts." Wind shear – a sudden, violent change in wind speed and direction – can tear apart a light aircraft. I wondered what wind shear would do to our heavy ship. The downdraft, another mountain ogre, is an invisible wave of air so strong that it can force a plane into the ground. Fortunately, only the aircraft died in the wreckage.

That afternoon the Chinook planned to cruise slowly for two hours alongside bare rock cliffs and over drifts of snow-burdened spruce in the four-mile-square search area. Emergency signals from the civilian plane were being picked up on electronic directional finders built into the aircraft, though most signals were bouncing off mountain walls and snow-packs, adding only confusion. From Chinook windows we would seek a small, white plane lying on a white snowdrift, concealed under a fresh white snowfall, in an awesome, white mountainous world without end. Not easy for the human eye.

The single-engine Mooney had been piloted by Truman, a 72-year-old man from Hotchkiss, Colorado, who had flown Civil Air Patrol search missions for 50 years. His business-trip passenger, Craig, was a 35-year-old man, also of Hotchkiss. Tuesday morning at 8:20 they had taken off from Salida, after waiting Monday night for winds to subside, and flown west to cross the Divide. "Bottom of clouds is at twelve thousand five hundred feet," the pilot radioed back to Salida Airport. "We're at sixteen thousand four hundred feet on top of clouds. We're going over." Radio contact then ceased. Fifteen minutes later a jetliner flying overhead heard an emergency transmitter over the Divide, and a search was launched.

Entering the Chinook for the search flight, Mel told our team, "The pilots will be doing some demanding flying in these winds. We've got to take some weight off. Get unnecessary gear out of the fuselage. Most of the crew will stay behind. Only five El Paso people plus myself will go, along with two Rocky Mountain Rescue men." So three of us could not fly – a difficult decision for Mel, but that's what leaders are for.

I was confused by the co-pilot's words to me that morning, which credited our landing to the great weight of a Chinook. Now, in the same winds, we were reducing the weight to the bare mininum. Much time later I learned that the weight isn't the problem; in fact, a heavier ship is more stable in flight, as compared to a lighter aircraft that bounces around. Instead, the problem is a matter of power – the morning flight was in cold air with greater air density, therefore allowing for greater engine power than in the afternoon, with its warmer air.

Mel asked for volunteers to leave the chopper.

Dick, a mellow and seasoned member, and Mike Sheldon, a radio expert, offered, but Mel replied, "No, I may need you." Then two new members volunteered, gathered their gear and went down the ramp.

"I'll leave. I'm a woman and kind of old," I said quietly, trying not to sound like a martyr.

Mel paused, deep in thought, then turned to Ed, our youngest member, always full of eagerness for every mission. "I'm going to ask you to leave, Ed. Peggy is in better shape than you are."

"Oh, no. Now he won't love me any more," I blurted out. Much laughter relieved the strain.

Ed, his black eyes flashing, said privately to Mel, "I want to go!" I remembered the winds near Cyclone Mountain that tossed the Chinook through the air. I would have been happy to remain on the ground.

The clouds flew from North Fork's basin when our chopper drew near. Two hours' search time isn't much, but it's customary and about all the pilots can handle in winds and peaks. We twisted around on the canvas benches to admire three boundaries for the search: Mount Shavano at 14,229 feet guarding from the north; a curved saddle between Mount Aetna at 13,771 feet, and Taylor Mountain at 13,657 feet hemming in the south; and the Continental Divide snaking along at 13,000 feet on the west ridge. These peaks, as well as 14,197-foot Mount Princeton to the north, are parts of an eroded tertiary batholith (formerly molten lava) stretching 20 miles in width.

In a small, flat patch of snow far up in the basin, the two Rocky Mountain Rescue men jumped from the ramp carrying a directional finder. Trudging on snowshoes, they would radio readings back to the Civil Air Patrol in base, who needed clearer signals than aircraft were picking up.

I brightened under the sunshine and felt that the extreme winds were diminishing and that the missing Mooney and two survivors would soon be seen from our Chinook windows. But all we saw were search snowmobiles zooming over the snowcrust. Then suddenly the winds were more severe than before, bouncing the chopper up, then forcing it down under a niagara of air.

The Chinook isn't designed for searching from its windows; any searcher who glues his forehead to a window is unable to wear a seat belt – unless it's over his calves. While I studied the spruce below for broken tree trunks – the telltale sign of a crash landing – I was also clutching the bench to keep from tumbling to the floor. Although my cramped leg fell asleep, my mind stayed alert, eyes roving over the sparse, white forest for something unusual. A crash never looks like a crash. We look for something unnatural in the terrain, like a straight line, which stands out in the curves of nature. We watch for the broken tops of timber sheared off by a low-flying aircraft. We check out terrain that's disturbed. We are alert for scorched patches from a fuel burn. A flash of metal or color is immediately visible. Our eyes keep moving.

By now I've worked several searches and their wreckage. None are the same. Aircraft crash at different angles, and on gentle to steep slopes, and at varying speeds; the results range from an almost intact fuselage to a crushed soda can. Set against a mountain made of rocks and trees, many are invisible in a fly-by.

Twice the ship wandered close against imposing cliffs. Too close for me. With each cliff I heard the two motors snarl under full power. Loud vibrations caused the fuselage to shudder in agony. A severe wind can surge up a mountain slope in an "updraft"; then can roll down the opposite side, the lee side, with unbelievable velocity in a "downdraft," sometimes dropping thousands of feet per minute. All this strength can't be seen, only felt.

After the unsuccessful search was over, we retrieved the two Rocky Mountain Rescue men from a meadow in the basin and landed on the runway. While walking to the terminal, I put my arm across the shoulders of the co-pilot, David Sanders, and said, "Tell your wife you're one hell of a fine pilot."

"We almost bought it twice," he made clear, shaking his head from side to side. "The downdrafts were too strong." I was the only searcher who naively believed the pilots were close to the cliffs by choice – others knew we were near crashing. "Those six hundred pounds of people and gear we left behind," the crew chief explained, "may have made the difference between crashing and not crashing."

While standing on a 12,000-foot ridge at the foot of Taylor Mountain, the Rocky Mountain Rescue men had picked up a strong, direct signal from an emegency transmitter somewhere high above. But by the time we got them back on board, the sun was too low for continued searching. Once the Chinook was tethered on the runway for the night, pilots and crew relaxed in the terminal, while we were driven to Salida for dinner.

Peter Peelgrane, a Channel 7 helicopter pilot still in the air looking for the Mooney, had heard on the radio of the strong signals from Taylor Mountain. He flew across Taylor's north face, and at 6 o'clock in a setting sun caught a glint of something shiny. "I circled around to see what it was, but the sun had gone behind a cloud. I wasn't able to make out anything. But when the sun came out again I spotted it," Peter remembered. "I got to within fifty feet of the wreckage, but saw no signs of life. Winds were gusting to sixty miles per hour, so I couldn't land or stay around."

The long day had ended with this discovery of a second wreckage – a jumbled wad of metal sitting in a ringside seat for the frantic search that had been going on 2,000 feet below in the basin. We had not flown high enough.

2 way radio

Marooned at a restaurant, we received word on our radios. The Chinook pilots and crew, still in the terminal, ran to their tied-down aircraft to fly to the site and check for any survivors perhaps not sighted by the TV chopper.

Darkness was near when the helicopter's front wheels lightly touched the knife-edge saddle, its back suspended over air. Three men had jumped from the door, when a wind hit suddenly, and the Chinook thundered instantly into the air, taking the fourth jumper along. The three hurried over rocks and snow to the crash, where they found two dead and no survivors. They returned to the saddle, where the ship scooped them off the rocks before the wind and night could wrap cold arms around their bodies and hold them until dawn.

Early in the morning, in 12 hours, the crew of two, plus seven from the El Paso team, two from Alpine Rescue, and two from the National Transportation and Safety Board would assist Captain Ron in the body recoveries. I hoped that the drama of this first day, and worry over my ability to mess up after only six months in the group, wouldn't prevent sleep.

The air in the small terminal was hot and stale, so two fellows and I threw our pads and down-filled bags on the runway and reveled in 10-degree temperatures. Rolling over in my mummy bag during the still night, I gazed lovingly at the nearby Chinook resting on the runway under the haunting reflection from a full moon. The three blades of each rotor were tethered to the earth with cables, to prevent it from sneaking away into space. How could I have ever thought it was built from spare parts? This enchanting ship, looking so alien to our planet, was a spirit, not a means of transportation.

At daylight the terminal filled with an endless parade of men, from the Federal Aviation Administration through the Civil Air Patrol to media. My eyes looked only to Captain Ron, who stood on a chair briefing those of us who were to make the recoveries. The entire room listened intently.

"We'll be sixteen – two pilots, two crew, twelve rescuers." I would be the only woman and had better not make a mistake. I was too visible – and so was the load of years I carried on my face. I know that any slip can jeopardize a misson, or my neck.

"At the saddle you'll get the signal to go. Get out fast. It's thirteen thousand. Pilots can only hover for seconds." The crowd was tense, almost grim, unsettling me. "If winds kick up and the helicopter can't come back and get us, we'll weight the bodies with rocks to prevent wind from blowing them down the snowfield into Hunkydory Gulch. Then climb down and hike out. We'll come back and get them another day."

The air was calm, our ride smooth. The pilots approached the knife-edge saddle at agonizing slowness while we sat motionless inside. Then rock and snow appeared outside the window. Captain Ron jumped up to fling open the door. Rescuers flew out. I was last – no gentlemen aboard.

Needles blasted my face. As my boot left the bottom step, the deafening rotors, slicing the air close over my head, rose heavily away from the saddle. On the ground, through the white-out, I saw our group huddled downslope 30 feet away. The rescuer running before me was off to one side, and since speed in getting out of rotor-blade range is of utmost importance, I dove on my belly across the crust and skidded into the group. My ingenuity saved seconds. Once the aircraft had lifted and banked, we slowly stood up. "Are you all right, Peggy?" Captain Ron called.

"Sure!" What was the matter with him?

"Thought you got hit by a rotor when you flew through the air." We laughed together and my tension relaxed.

The co-pilot complimented us later on our flight out the door. "Never saw twelve people leave an aircraft so fast." We could have gone out the rear ramp even more rapidly except that it was hanging a daunting 40 feet in the air.

We could see the wreckage protruding above the mountain's rocky profile, less than a quarter mile ahead at a slightly higher elevation. Easy, except for the sharp ebony rocks we balanced on, with the corn snow between deep and unknown – perhaps hiding a bone fracture.

The wind had taken its gusts elsewhere; a frozen silence was left in the air. Our eyes saw the earth below with ice-water clarity. My face was pleasantly numb, although the below-zero temperature made my jaw stiff. As on other body recoveries, rescuers were mute, without expression, concentrating on their assigned task.

Mel turned to Peter Westcott, a quiet and conscientious new member. "Go with Peggy. Look around the rocks for anything important, like body parts." We circled but found only business papers and a cowboy boot. I watched for plane parts, for I couldn't believe a single-engine Mooney had smashed into such a small size. Returning to the site I realized the nose was folded under the fuselage, with wings upright. The tail had curled around and shielded the emergency transmitter fastened inside, causing signals to beam down the mountainside in a narrow range. The aircraft, flying east, had caught the mountain slope only 600 feet below the summit – perhaps winds were chasing the pilot back to the runway, or he had gone into a spin.

While carrying the boot and papers back to the site, I noticed a body covered with a soft blanket of snow, lying on its back over the rocks. I was shocked, even though we had expected to find a pilot and his passenger. Someone brushed away the snow, and I inhaled deeply. He wore an expression of great surprise across his handsome, ruddy face. Had he seen the mountain looming ahead in his last seconds?

I was looking at him mournfully, thinking of his family, when a breeze drifted across the mountain and brushed back his wavy red hair. The illusion of life bewildered me.

He lay in an ancient cathedral, its walls the enduring peaks nearby. His Maker watched over him while his eyes stared into the sky. Now we came to place him in a dreadful, black plastic bag and lift him away from his mountain eyrie . . . hard to understand why.

Body bags are not large. I wondered how we could bring his outstretched frozen arms and legs close to his body. I whispered to Dick, "How do we do this?"

"Here, let me show you. You turn him on his side. Then you lean on his limbs." I wasn't too familiar with handling death, but somehow I kept calm, and realized for the first time that my passage through life had been sheltered from the act of dying.

Actually, the body bag was a liner with flimsy handles and fragile zipper attached to thin plastic. Our passenger was a large man and the route to the Chinook landing zone traversed difficult rocks. I hoped the bag wouldn't rip.

Five of us took positions at handles. Our sixth – Tom Fiore, from Alpine Rescue – was unscrewing electronic gear in the crushed cabin, which I thought strange in the intense cold, and for a pilot who couldn't care. After the mission Tom told me the gear was removed for the FAA, which would be investigating the cause of the crash. I saw later in a photo that the pilot lay close by, partly in the cockpit. I had never glanced around for him. I had already seen plenty.

Even with several short rest stops while carrying our bur-
den, we still arrived panting at the saddle. To keep rotor wash
from blowing the bodies down the slope, we dug a ledge for
them in the snow with our boots. When the other team had
carried over the pilot's body, we were ready for pick-up.
Captain Ron radioed the Chinook waiting below.

I was first to hunker down as low as possible in the snow –
out of rotor-blade reach – and clench the body-bag handle, for
I saw coming toward us a black aircraft suspended in space
like a frozen raven, its tiny feet hanging, soaring slowly to
our site.

For a speedy entry into the fuselage we needed the front
door close to the body bags. With the rotor blades whirling
over our prone figures, I was overwhelmed, filled with adrenaline. Rotor winds and deafening noise beat on us. A mael-
strom of ice flakes flew in a white-out. We would be second
to enter the aircraft. My eyes watched the boot heel before my
face; when it moved, I rose and strained to lift the handle.
Five of us rapidly hauled the body to the open door. A
crewman, leaning out, grabbed the bag and, with three bearers
in front helping, hoisted it up steep and narrow steps, while
before my horrified eyes the body's frozen feet pierced the
plastic and emerged to the knees.

A sudden grip on my shoulder from the crewman and a
violent push on my rear from Tom, the last rescuer, cata-
pulted me into the fuselage, where I landed on the floor without dignity. Before I could climb onto a bench and belt, the
Chinook was aloft and banking steeply toward the airport.
We were back on the runway two hours after lift-off.

Morticians on the runway took charge while we watched
quietly from inside our ship. I felt resentment that strangers
took possession of our pilot and passenger, for these weren't
unknown men in a common accident in an ordinary place.
Instead, the madness of a great storm had dragged down this
skilled pilot from his sky, forcing the mountain landing from
which no take-off for pilot or passenger or aircraft was ever
again to be.

8. BRIBERY

*A search can be clothed in fierce storms, haunted
nights, unexpected bivouacs, deafening winds and
chilling rains − or under extraordinary conditions
of beauty.*

"Grab the tail of Sally there in front. She'll pull
you up the trail," an outfitter on horseback called to
me through thick mist.

Only a fool hangs on to a horse's tail. Just to sneak
behind the muscular legs, to reach out and grab a handful of
wiry hair terrified me. But good old Sally didn't kick, so I held
on with both hands whenever the trail rose steeply over the
four miles atop the Continental Divide. Arriving at Sawtooth
Mountain, where our trail left the Divide, I stepped forward
to thank Sally, who to my astonishment, had two enormous
ears. I had been pulled out by a mule.

This September mission, during my third summer on the
team, was based nine miles north of Wolf Creek Pass, in the
heart of the San Juan Range in southern Colorado. At low elevations, around 10,000 feet, the valleys in this range were
cluttered with debris from rock avalanches, but a lush, almost
tropical plant growth crowded over the moist earth. Above
the trees the alpine ridges were gentle, no higher than 12,400

feet, and a crust of low grasses, instead of barren stones, blanketed their rising and falling slopes.

The mission, a search, had closed in tragedy the previous afternoon when the body of a bow-hunting Minnesota doctor had been found by a search collie in a shallow ravine three miles from base. Despite cloudcover and drizzle and wind during the night, we expected to hear, at dawn, the deep moan of our Chinook echoing up the valley. However, the helicopter commander, still in Durango, radioed Tom Fiore, a bright-eyed and golden-bearded field leader from the Alpine Rescue team: "We can't fly. Weather's bad. Feel terrible leaving you all there." This wasn't the first time rescuers had flown in and hiked out.

Although I worried about the fast uphill pace of 42 young searchers from six rescue teams (Larimer, Alpine, Arapahoe, El Paso, Western State and Mineral), seven Utah tracking dogs and their handlers, four outfitters on horseback who had packed in the bow-hunters and were now packing out the camp with mules, I urged Tom, "Let's go. Let's go. If we wait any longer the weather might clear. Then the Chinook will come and we won't be able to hike the trail."

"Yeah, I agree. We'll leave this morning at eleven."

And so began our long march over the Divide, stalwart spine of our country. Grey clouds hugged the earth, obscuring the trail and swallowing the front of the line. We followed like Indians along the narrow, deeply rutted path. I thought of elk and deer, horses and pack mules that had walked the trail since long ago – many obviously not housebroken. Wind gusts threatened my balance. Snow pellets flung from clouds stung my face. Icy blasts drove dense 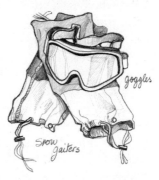 patches of white clouds, like vapors from hell, out of deep valleys to vanish beside us. This autumn storm excited me with its unruly vigor, its raw power and its deep cry that forced our silence.

I turned and squinted at Daniel, the overly prepared El Paso rescuer behind me, who was hidden inside goggles, face mask, hood, gloves – not a patch of skin exposed – and missing the unique strength of this awesome storm on a 12,000-foot ridge. Normal people don't venture through high country in a tempest; they postpone or cancel their trip. Only rescuers or an odd fisherman risk the weather and brave the violent tempers and fits that enthrall a true mountaineer.

When chilling winds rage, animals and birds can retreat to nearby valleys, but plants have no legs or wings. As we hiked along the Divide, I noticed that the green grasses and alpine flowers which blanket a summer tundra had now withered to pale gold, their foliage and flower heads bowed low, submitting to the lacerating winds of the Divide. Fringed gentians, vibrant blue against the ice crystals, bloomed in scattered colonies, with an occasional alpine sunflower, still yellow in autumn.

I watched the storm's sharp cutting edge prune back summer's growth on ancient Engelmann spruce trees only three feet high. The blast of ice particles against my cheek also blasted twisted trunks of fallen spruce, tortured by wind even when dead. These trees chose to grow on the Divide rather than in a protected niche below, just as I preferred to walk this blustery trail rather than ride a sheltering helicopter.

During the mission we had climbed back to camp late at night to eat supper and fall into our bags, too tired for sleep. Nevertheless, I now stood on the Divide beside Sawtooth Mountain and smiled to see that our route would continue for another nine miles.

"Hey look, fella, we've nothing to do all afternoon but follow that trail out the valley," I rejoiced to a searcher.

"But I've got blisters on both feet," he groaned.

The trail – all downhill, thank God – zigzagged 2,000 feet to a sheltered valley enlivened by Hope Creek rushing to the Rio Grande. In the valley floor I lost control in a primeval scene that looked like the dawn of creation. Spongy moss covered the bare ground and rotting trunks of fallen trees. The creek ran so fast it made me dizzy. But best of all, rattlesnake orchids, taller than I had ever seen, bloomed with abandon for miles along the wide path. Savage wind and penetrating cold had remained on the Divide; in the valley we enjoyed a heavy, green-tinted rain.

My lungs expanded with countless gulps of cold air. My arms and legs swung like a metronome, in a repetition that drained away stress and tiredness. My boots soared over the trail. The reward for joining the mission, bribing me to come again, was this remarkable five-hour display of weather over a path so close to heaven.

Yet a persuasive bribe from Mother Nature doesn't always demand hiking – though it might require scrutiny and patience. It can be a glimpse into the simple life of a daring mammal, an enchanting rodent or a skillful bird. For this glimpse, a searcher must stop, look around and blend in. Peak baggers, agile and young and wearing blinders, ascend a mountain rapidly, seeing only the summit. Their descent – in the Rockies, frequently hurried by afternoon lightning bolts – becomes a race to their camp or car for the sheer joy of speed. I lived in this whirl most of my life, unaware that the plodding tortoise had a good point.

My headstrong attitude changed during my first summer in rescue work when we were looking for a missing climber on Mount Aeolus, in the Needle Mountains of the San Juan Range, 25 miles north of Durango in southwestern Colorado. During a dawn briefing the second day, our field leader said, "Mike, set up a radio relay on the ridge between Aeolus and North Aeolus. Take Peggy with you." Me? I knew the location was at a heady 13,800 feet, so was relieved to hear, "The Chinook will drop you both off somewhere below the ridge."

Simply put, a radio relay is a team of one or two people who perch high on a mountain above a mission to extend the communication range or to transmit messages back and forth between teams on one side of the mountain and base on the other. Radio waves won't pass through the mountain, nor will they bend over it. Being on a relay isn't easy; brief messages received by ear and dispatched by mouth are no problem, but long messages that ramble on and on – and must be repeated exactly as said, in every detail – cause my mind to rebel.

With a 200-foot coil of rope across my shoulder and a heavy radio in Mike's grip, we climbed to our position after the helicopter drop-off. We each sat on a rock in the frigid morning air, with the radio at Mike's side, waiting for team and base transmissions to begin. "Now we can rest and peak-gaze," I said. Mike is impressive – big and blond on the outside, quiet and controlled on the inside. A good companion.

"I never would have come here by myself. Too lonely," Mike offered.

Solitude appeals to me.

I was intently examining the east face of Aeolus, a steep slope of narrow ledges, when I was startled to see a climber in a white shirt standing by the sharp summit.

"Mike. Our missing climber was wearing white."

"This is relay. Someone's on the summit in white," Mike called to base.

"Yes. A mountain goat! Searchers have already fixed binoculars on him," base replied.

Soon three goats (true goats don't exist in the Rockies – ours is a primitive goat-antelope) stood like statuary beside the 14,084-foot mountain summit, a mass of stone with no green foliage to eat or rainwater to drink. They admired the view, just like climbers at the top. Two vanished to the west, but the other goat moved in our direction, downclimbing cautiously over sheer rock walls between crumbling ledges. Soon he sat on a grassy ledge to survey stark peaks and raucous waterfalls that dropped from high basins. When two searchers moved along our ridge and started for the summit, I watched carefully, deaf to Mike and the radio relay, to see the goat's reaction. The east face of Aeolus had room for three; however, when the men were close the mountain goat rose slowly and boldly defied gravity by plunging over the near-vertical rock slabs. Training kids must be a harrowing experience for a nanny. When this sightseeing goat reached the beginning of our knife-edge ridge, he disappeared from our view.

yellow bellied marmot

A yellow-bellied marmot, whose chocolate droppings I had noticed around my boots, peered over his nose to watch me sitting by his vegetable garden, a bouquet of edible tundra

flowers. He seemed bewildered by my presence on his sun-
ning rock; I wasn't a marmot – he could tell – but then why
did I sit there?

While Mike continued to relay messages across the mountain, I discovered a friendly flock of brown-capped rosy finches flying around us; whenever a butterflylike insect fluttered
out into space, a finch swooped down to terminate it in one
snap. Swallows carved elegant figure-eights above our perch
while chipmunks scurried past, oblivious to Mike's voice.
The mountain was alive with far more than the efforts of our
search.

"Peggy, you take over the radio for a while," Mike said.

My mind snapped back from far away. Taking Mike's radio
position, I was frustrated to see the goat picking his way steadily along our ridge top. To relay radio messages is travail
enough without being diverted by the approach of a furry
ghost – with large black eyes, a wet black nose and curved
black horns. Ten feet away he stopped and we faced off. Goat
sexes look alike, especially to me at 14,000, though by looking
deeply into the warm and expressive eyes, I realized he was a
nanny. The two lady mountaineers hesitated, honoring each
other's space but locked in suspense. The nanny then turned
and with non-skid hoofs that splayed wide, she carefully
edged off the ridge, disappearing from my sight. No rappel
rope, no belay. Just traction pads, short legs and true bravery.

Morning was already lost to afternoon, when a brief message closed the search. Mike and I held the ridge until all
teams were on their way to base by foot or chopper. Before
leaving I swept the peaks with my eyes. "Mike, look! That persistent goat is sitting above us on the summit. See the snow
cornice?" Only her nose and eyes, like three chunks of coal,
stood out from the overhanging lip of snow. Later, while
plodding across a soft snowfield to come off the mountain, I
gazed back often to see her reigning from the poetic setting on
North Aeolus.

The bribery for a mission isn't always an admirable and
appealing mountain goat. In fact, I haven't seen a goat since.
More often we are induced to volunteer for the next labori-
ous search by recalling impressive moments from previous
ones; usually of simple beauty or possible danger, they etch
themselves into our minds. It is those scenes that we bring

back so often that, in time, the actual victim, the reason for
the mission, fades away.

This occurred some years ago when, before my time, our
team struggled on the face of Pikes Peak to lift a hypothermic
75-year-old man in a litter through waist-deep snow to a rescue Chinook – only to arrive just as an electrical storm broke
overhead. Team members still describe with rolling eyes the
brilliant lightning that lit up the metal helicopter. They
vociferously demonstrate the thunderclaps that crashed overhead for two hours before take-off was safe. In retelling the
terror of this story, our members always ignore the unfortunate elderly victim and his hypothermia. The powerful
storm has become the villain – and the vamp that beguiles
members to return.

In my mind, the most memorable missions combine a grati-
fying rescue with the wonder of nature. A humble wonder
will do; it needn't be startling. More vivid to me now than
the sprained ankle we rescued one night, are the crisp
shadows on the trail – members hiking without headlamps
during an evening drenched in moonlight. Or the hot-pink
smoke that billowed from a popped smoke cannister rising
above a wintry pine forest at twilight to guide a helicopter to
a victim – a victim now dim in my mind, leaving only the
smoke. And a midnight on Pikes Peak, at 14,000 feet, when a
rock hole hiding under an ancient snowpack grabbed my leg,
and I fell, halting my rapid descent – only to look out and realize that the splash of red, yellow and white stars blinking in a
sky was actually my town on the plains. When bored in the
city I flash such memories across my mind.

Some missions have no beauty. Instead, they are adven-
tures soaked in pain. No smiles, no laughter, no gratification.
This was the case one late December night, when Andy, a
strong and mature 33-year-old engineer visiting from Illinois,
left the icy face of Pikes Peak at 2:00 in the afternoon, for Barr
Camp, five miles away, to obtain help for Hugh, his climbing
companion and a caretaker at the camp. Hugh Walkup was
sitting with a fractured fibula at 13,500 feet. When night came
but help didn't, Hugh slid, hopped and crawled over ice and
crust, pulling himself along by his ice axe, until he reached
Barr Camp late that evening. Andy, unfamilar with the
mountain, had vanished.

Our team – three women (Betsy Laubhan, an Air Force nurse; Selena Vaughn, rarely on a mission; and myself) and four men (Rich, the leader, Mel, Rudy and Kevin) – drove the winding road to the 14,110-foot summit and stepped out of two four-wheel-drive vehicles into a ferocious storm. Gale winds swept across the blackness, causing us to stagger while our clothes snapped around us alarmingly. The smallest effort left us panting. Our little caravan crouched behind six-foot snow drifts which had been blown into stone-hard sculptures by wind. Still the fury found us, numbing exposed hands in seconds. We had worked on our equipment and clothing far too long, as though afraid to leave our mothers – the vehicles. We felt like victims ourselves. When we could stall our departure no longer, we fought our way across the summit plateau to the track of the cog train to the summit, which was swept free of snow by the force of the wind. Our boots clung to the mountain gravel between the ties while, from behind, a frozen devil drove our bodies.

A quarter mile down the track we branched off over rocks embedded in ice until the top of the face stopped us. In all we had covered probably only a half-mile from the vehicles. Seemed like a marathon. We struck our ice axes into the thick sheet of diamond-hard ice, splintering it. I stared down the steep, slick slope through the bitter darkness and felt the chill of fear. A slip

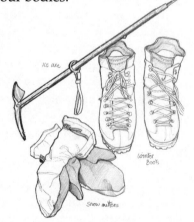

Ice axe

Winter Boots

Snow mittens

meant a wild 2,500-foot ride over ice and projecting rocks. I wouldn't descend the face to search for Andy, absolutely not. Before Rich asked us what we thought, I shouted into his ear, "Too dangerous. Packs are heavy. Ice too hard for self-arrest." The others agreed, so the decision was made to return to the vehicles. Somewhere on the lower slopes, or below treeline, a man was lost in zero temperatures, without food or shelter, and pursued by a wind that howled itself hoarse.

Turning around we were thrown back by an invisible wall of wind. Ice crystals flew into my squinting eyes, mingling with wind tears. My wool balaclava, heavy with frozen

breath, slipped down to expose my nose, which caught frostbite. My headlamp lit uneven ice and crude rocks, but I could
hardly see with what I thought were frozen eyeballs.

We finally reached the cog railroad tracks again, and started
back up to the summit. My pack became a sail that threatened
to lift me into the night. In panic I dropped to my knees and
clutched the cog rail with one hand as I crawled up the slope.
While in that strange position, Rudy, made of meat and muscle, came from behind with Betsy hooked on his arm. Bending over, he lifted me to my feet and I hugged his other arm.
We were the last three to slowly struggle up the track, gasping
in the thin air, bodies huddled together but remote from each
other.

Two hours of high hell in paralyzing wind and penetrating
cold left me immune to any beauty the night had. However,
my sensuous side remained intact, for when I lurched across
the summit to enter a vehicle and felt the windless air, tears
of joy flooded my eyes. I felt profound comfort and safety in a
womb of steel, rocked to sleep by powerful gusts while listening to a lullaby sung by wind seeping through door cracks.

The water in our canteens was frozen and a fire impossible.
Of our two vehicles, one contained a battery that died at zero;
the other had diesel fuel that congealed at zero. We sat
through the long night, cramped in sleeping bags, until a
pink dawn stilled the wind and brought warmth to the battery. The diesel, still congealed, was abandoned, like our victim below.

After leaving Hugh, Andy was halfway down the frozen
face when he remembered being told to always stay well to
the left of the A-frame, a shelter at treeline, so as not to miss
Barr Trail, which led to Barr Camp, where help was available.
The trail was buried under snow but still visible as an opening through the trees. Andy stayed left of the A-frame so far
that he went off the face, over a round ridge, and into a gla-
cier-formed bowl, the Bottomless Pit, which forms the 2,500-
foot north face of Pikes Peak. By then bitter darkness covered
the peak and the bowl, which is known for winds that screech
like a jet stream. Andy was warmly dressed with hat, gloves,
shirt, trousers, socks and underwear all of wool, a down coat
and leather boots. But he carried no food or water. Although
water flowed out of the bowl from under the snow and ice,

he didn't think to break through with his boot. He survived the night in the open, 2,500 feet below us, by hugging his knees while crouched on a rock bare of snow.

The next day Andy studied treeline below the vast bowl walls, seeking the A-frame or Barr Trail, both two miles away and out of sight. He didn't believe his compass. Ashamed to be confused and feeling his rescue was unnecessary, he hid under trees when the Chinook searched overhead. During his second night of crouching on a rock, Andy's situation became critical. He suffered more hunger and thirst, causing him to slip into mild hypothermia.

With the frigid dawn, Andy gave up trying to find the A-frame and Barr Trail. Determined to survive, he knew he must hike off the mountain immediately. Picking his way down the trailless South Fork of French Creek, which drains the Bottomless Pit, Andy heard at noon the voices of a search team looking for his body. He called to them and our frantic hunt was over.

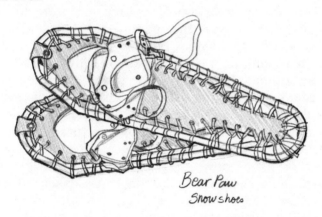

Bear Paw
Snow shoes

Any night as agonizing as that summit night is too large a price to pay for a mission. The painful experience forever bonded our team of seven, but for me, once was enough. Even so, I vividly remember the May following Andy's mission. We were on Pikes Peak for an injured cross-country skier, when I was finally rewarded for all the pain endured on prior missions.

I began the late Sunday afternoon rescue in shame. The bash team, which is sent out first to reach a victim, was leaving the Peak toll gate for a 10-mile drive to Glen Cove, another glacier-carved bowl. I gathered my gear in a frenzy and eagerly leaped into the front seat, only to discover en route that my climbing harness, webbing and caribiners remained back in my truck. I was mortified at the prospect that the other members would find out. After three and a half years in the group, I had forgotten the most important mission items. They might say to me, "Too old now. Bye-bye."

We went on snowshoes across a thick crust covering three feet of soft snow and halfway down a wind-packed slope. Our victim, Ross, lay on bare dirt under a spruce tree half a mile west of Glen Cove. He lay with fractured ribs and a punctured lung, thanks to a rocky avalanche chute that had looked interesting to him and his skiing companion. Attempting to ski the glazed slope, he had missed a turn and tumbled violently, bouncing off the rocks and into the air.

Rod, an ambulance paramedic on our team, arrived and knelt next to Ross to insert an I.V. into a vein in his forearm. I was supporting Ross's back with my legs and was impressed that Rod made the difficult injection on the first try; veins shrink in severe temperature, making them hard to find, and Rod's bare hands were turning stiff and numb. Annie, a city firewoman on the team, palpated Ross's blood pressure. Blood pressure attempts under our conditions can be a disaster. Background noise like talking, shouting to the uphaul team, and questions fired back and forth cause distraction and make the sound of surging blood inaudible. An artery contracts in the cold and is harder to feel, and, of course, Ross was shocky from the lung collapse and internal bleeding. Oxygen from our pressurized tank passed through a tube to his nostrils. Ross, who was bundled in a special sleeping bag with zippers all around, was then carefully lifted into our snowsled, his oxygen tank by his side. The canvas flaps were tucked over him and laced down with nylon webbing. His I.V. was disconnected, since Rod felt Ross had had enough by then. (Rod carries an I.V. pump for situations where gravity flow isn't possible.) He inserted a heparin lock to prevent clotting at the tip, and would reattach the system after reaching the ambulance. Then the uphill journey began.

Mel had gone ahead to scout a return route, as our trail going in had traversed a curve around a slope that fell rapidly to one side. Taking Ross over the firm crust might prove tricky. Instead, Mel preferred an uphaul, which would be quite simple and effective – and exhausting to the men in the hip-deep snow. A hundred feet up the rocky snowslope an anchor rope was looped around a secure boulder and a pulley was attached with caribiners. The rope came up from the snowsled, went through the pulley and dropped back down to four or five members, who were attached to the rope with prusik loops. By leaning back, the force of their weight easily raised the loaded snowsled.

Prusik Knot

I glanced around for a job that would cam-ouflage my lack of climbing gear. Four extra pair of snowshoes lay on the snow, with an empty oxygen tank nearby. Skee rigged them over my pack, and I started for our rescue vehicle higher on the mountain. Passing Daniel, who was working on the sled-uphaul, I remarked how tired I was, having hiked all day in a rainstorm. Carrying the clumsy gear uphill left me beyond exhaus-tion, although we were only at 11,500 feet. I was slowly passing the uphaul crew when someone called to me, "Don't leave, Peggy, we may need you." I stiffened. With doubts of even reaching the vehicle with my load, how could I help them in the deep snow? I said nothing, watched for a while and then sneaked away up the slope.

After shedding my load and munching stale brownies, I felt a surge of energy and a pang of guilt. I returned to help. When I reached the spot where the team had been working with the sled, all 11, plus Ross, had disappeared. For a second I was mystified, not knowing their route. Then my isolation gave me shivers of joy. I didn't hurry to scout their snow-shoes and sled tracks, even though night had rolled over the mountain, dragging storm clouds along. I wanted a while alone in this stark, white scene guarded by dark, overbearing rocks. Let them work with Ross. I had found my bribery.

While I absorbed the desolation of our vast mountainside below the clouds and beyond human scale, a brilliant flash of yellow light lit all before me. For a half-second the snow and the rocks and the clouds and the night turned to gold, blind-ing me after the darkness. Muffled explosions thundered from a storm in summer over a mountain in winter. I slowly followed the sled track to a hillside above our vehicles and the ambulance, where Skee had set up a brake system to let down the litter. He asked me, "Where have you been?" I just smiled. I realized I had been captivated by a rare outburst over the earth, and gazed at Skee as though from a great distance – he seemed a stranger. The exquisite, lonely wonder of my storm was not for their ears.

With Ross lying safely in an ambulance, 12 rescuers huddled together in the darkness to briefly discuss what had gone right, what had gone wrong. Lightning and thunder had ceased, replaced by corn snow that poured from the clouds and adorned our heads and shoulders. I didn't listen to the men's mumbled voices around me for I was too tired to care.

In time, the memory of Ross will fade – but never the bursts of golden light, the rumbles of thunder on that magic night.

9. SEDUCTIVE MOUNTAIN

*The mountain lures the solo climber with gentle
cliffs, then steeper walls, and finally a bastille.
The climber is mesmerized. On his descent, the
mountain repels and the toll is paid.*

 Suddenly, after flying 25 miles up the Animas
River from Durango, a flank of sun-splashed rock
flashed close by my Chinook window. Then another. Both rose abruptly to summits I couldn't see,
summits that stood above raw cliffs, summits that were sculp-
tured by glaciers out of tan, white and brown Precambrian
granite. Brilliant green grass spilled down between the cliffs,
like a Swiss meadow gone crazy, and competed with the
blinding blue sky. I flattened my face against the window,
hungry for more. So these were the Needle Mountains of the
San Juan Range, bristling out of a green pincushion in southwestern Colorado.

This late July morning was during my first summer on the
team. We came to search for a missing climber in these inac-
cessible mountains without roads, towns or airfields. In 1882
a narrow-gauge train track was constructed nearby – from
Durango north to the mining town of Silverton. It threaded
through the Animas River gorge on skimpy ledges that hung
precariously over the river far below. Over the years the little

cars carried more than $150,000,000 worth of gold and silver out of Silverton, chugging close to the Needles on its way down to Durango. Today the locomotives haul cars full of tourists to Silverton, and mountain climbers to where the river is bridged – the trail head to these remote summits that puncture clouds.

Our chopper, never a lofty flyer, had flown low up the river until ranches, mesas and plateaus had ceased and dense ever-green forests covered the rolling land. Without warning, the pilots banked under a crest of soaring summits – three four-teeners standing alone (Aeolus, Sunlight and Windom), with other peaks just shy of 14,000 crowding along awesome battle-ments. We circled in the glacier-dug valley, Chicago Basin, that nested between the rock jewels. While the pilots checked out the terrain for a landing site, I saw waterfalls pour from lonely alpine basins, to streak through rich meadows and dis-appear under Engelmann spruce.

After landing, and with rotors still revolving, we stepped off the ramp onto a sodden meadow and felt the warmth of the sun's rays at 11,500 feet. The sharp air smelled of tundra, and I inhaled deeply. Looking beyond the wild flowers and Needle Creek which crowded beside our aircraft, I asked, "Where is this Aeolus, Ruler of the Winds?"

"Right above you," someone answered, "Almost three thousand feet of it. The summit's behind, out of sight."

Rescuers were gathering by the radio tent for a briefing. I collected sandwich-es, a soft drink and fruit from boxes sent up by the Red Cross, threw them in my daypack, and quickly joined the group. We stood with La Plata County rescuers and Outward Bound volunteers while a La Plata sheriff's deputy briefed us on the mission.

"We've got a missing Denver obstetri-cian, 62 years old, name of Larry. He's five foot nine inches, and one hundred forty-five pounds, has grey hair, wears elastic knee supports, carries a red fanny pack and a blue backpack, and uses a short shovel handle for a walking stick, which should have left holes in the snow-pack as a clue. On Monday he was climbing Aeolus with a friend, Van, who became tired, couldn't keep up. Van called, 'I'm going down!' across the grassy slope to Larry. Van doesn't know if Larry heard him, because Larry didn't answer, just continued up. Anyway he hasn't been seen since Monday morning – three days ago."

"What kind of a mountaineer is he?" a rescuer asked.

"Not experienced. Has no technical skills or gear. More a strong hiker. He's fast and very intense, according to his wife. Two years ago he took up climbing fourteeners and has done thirty-seven already. Van says Larry's a tenacious climber. Determined. Friday night when they drove down from Denver, Larry was exhausted from work. After a short motel rest, they both rode the narrow gauge train on Saturday. They got off at the bridge and hiked eight hours into Chicago Basin here. They camped at Twin Lakes, above the basin. Then on Sunday they climbed Sunlight and Windom. Monday was to be Aeolus."

After the briefing, while we hauled our gear from the aircraft, a string of horsemen, wearing hats with brims turned up on the sides, rode up the trail on sleek quarter horses.

"Who are they?" I asked a deputy.

"Colorado Mounted Rangers, volunteers from Durango. They're here to help. Van is with them."

When they had dismounted, one said, "We left our horse trailers at Purgatory ski resort. It's a four-hour ride up here. On the way we interviewed about a hundred campers, but nobody's seen the missing climber."

A conductor for the narrow gauge insisted that no one of Larry's description had flagged the train and ridden the river gorge to Durango. So Larry was on the mountain. We must find him.

Van, a relaxed and pleasant 34-year-old engineer, had hiked down the trail to the train on Tuesday and alerted the sheriff in Durango. He told me, "A pilot flew a fixed-wing aircraft all around Aeolus on Wednesday and didn't see a trace of Larry."

"Yes," I replied, "but searchers on foot see and hear better."

Our El Paso team of five – Mel, Chuck, Cory, Mike and I – was assigned to do a hasty search of Twin Lakes, a vast bench between stone cliffs at 12,000 feet, where Larry and Van had camped on Sunday. The rangers and Van would join us. The slim trail, still slippery from yesterday's downpour, soon steepened. To my dismay, a ranger said, "This is too much for the horses. We'll go back." Van received radio permission to continue with us, but I worried about the pot-belly that over-hung his belt; Mike, too, was a little heavy. Yet I knew full well that I had slowed with age; no doubt our speeds would be the same.

Mel and Chuck, fit and fast and experienced in the moun-tains, led up the trail. An abundance of water from summer snowmelt gushed over tilted slabs of rock, in the middle of which lay our submerged trail. Lavender and blue and purple columbine drifted at the rock edge. Gross leaves and massive, white flower heads of cow pars-nip menaced our route, while violets, heavily in bloom, hid the soaked earth. Too opulent for me; I longed for the restraint of the tundra.

Columbine

Above treeline, where tempera-tures are too cold for tree growth, Van felt the elevation and slowed his pace. Up ahead, Chuck turned his reddish beard our way and urged, "Hurry up! We've got to move faster or we'll never get there."

While the six of us were still on the trail – now pitched so steeply that we clutched plants to aid in our ascent – word came by radio from the Alpine Rescue Team: "We've got Larry's blue backpack at the twelve-thousand-foot level on the south ridge. Probably not far from where he was when Van shouted up to him." A climber never leaves a pack behind; then he has no water, food or rain clothing if he's injured or caught by storm. The team laid orange flagging in a wide rectangle around the pack – a warning against touch-ing. The scent was preserved for a tracking dog, to be flown with its handler from Durango.

"Send Van back," base radioed. "You five continue up to Twin Lakes. The Chinook will get you for a drop-off at the pack."

We climbed up to the bench and stared at an immense snowfield, obviously deep and mushy, smothering whatever was underneath. Two lakes, covered with blue ice, broke through the snow to complete the bleak winter scene – on the last days of July. We gingerly crossed the snowfield, dreading the sudden crashes through snow crust, until bare ground appeared around a crumbling mining cabin. While Chinook-waiting, I walked along the melting snow edge, brilliant yellow with snow buttercup. I feared that the roots of the alpine flowers, still dormant under three feet of snow, wouldn't sprout all summer; sun warmth might never reach their beds. New snow would be falling in four weeks. What a sleep!

I pondered a quick snooze myself, when base radioed, "The pilot says slope by pack is too steep. Hike over."

Dropping off the bench we traversed below a cirque packed cliff-to-cliff with another melting snowfield. The ground was soggy with running water, and when we forced our way through thick willows higher than our heads, miniature cascades hiding among the roots caused our boots to slip. Since Mel and Chuck had ice axes, they climbed into the snow-packed cirque above us and explored the deep crack where snow had melted away from the warm rock cliff – where a body falling from the 500-foot parapet above might be hidden.

Mel called on the radio, "Search up here with us."

"Not without ice axes," said Mike, ever conservative. "It's safer to go around the base of the southeast ridge."

I'm glad I didn't argue. Later I was shocked to hear that their route across the ridge was between two towering rock walls only feet apart that harbored a narrow and steep trench of snow. As they climbed higher, the snow became ice. Without crampons they were soon forced to stay off the ice, and to climb by jamming their feet flat against the walls – a dangerous spread-eagle. Having gone that far, they were committed;

ice crampon

return was impossible. The men cautiously struggled up, because to go down was more dangerous. I would have died of fright – if not from a fall.

During the afternoon the helicopter swept close to rocky

ramparts on Aeolus in pursuit of Larry. Observers sighted a prone body covered by a white garment. Hopeful, Mike and I stopped in the willows and listened to radio traffic. When the pilots hovered closer, rotor wash blew the garment down the wall, leaving only an illusion. A searcher rescued it – a turtle-neck from Sears. Had it belonged to Larry? A call to his wife in Denver was negative. "He owned nothing from Sears," she said. Later, a metal canteen picked up by another searcher gave us hope, until Van claimed the doctor carried a plastic hospital bottle.

Rounding the southeast ridge, Mike and I came upon a giant reflector oven, made of rock walls and dry gravel soil, tilted to absorb the searing rays of a mid-summer sun. Flowers of rich gold and lemon yellow, with intense blue and cool white for contrast, crowded in the oven. "Let's have another lunch here," I suggested. The alpine-flower tapestry was exquisite and blocked out the search in my mind.

Afterwards we walked carefully across the deep grass on the slippery slopes until our eyes caught the blue backpack, ringed with orange flagging, lying on the verdant hill. To my distress, the site looked like a grave.

Base told us to continue searching higher. Hundreds of blue chiming bells had taken over the grass on the slope above, and I began climbing to them. Reveling in the waist-deep flowers, I suddenly heard a scream. "Rock! Rock!" A large stone was bounding down the mountain, straight for me. I hardened my muscles, ready to leap. At the last second, it veered away, leaving me with a racing heart. Mike (who says few words, and always softly) and I repeated the piercing warning as the missile continued down for 2,000 feet, just missing base in the valley. That night Mel admitted, "I loosened the stone while climbing, and watched in horror as it hurled down toward you."

While sunshine still lingered on the summits, teams came off the mountain. Moving slowly down, possessed by my thoughts of the mission, I hardly noticed the Chinook from Durango circling the camp. But when I saw a spirited blood-hound and its handler walk off the ramp, I became alert and moved briskly down toward base. I must see the bloodhound. I didn't realize Mel had offered to fly with the handler and dog to Twin Lakes and guide both, via our route, to the pack. Before I reached base, the three were in the chopper and aloft.

The pack contained underwear recently worn by Larry, which gave a scent to the bloodhound. But Larry's track away from the pack and up the mountain was cold. In good weather a scent lies in dense grass and dirt pockets for days, and can easily be traced by a tracking dog with his incredible sense of smell. But this time, wind and rain during the two previous afternoons had erased the scent entirely.

After the dog attempts, the helicopter flew up to take them aboard; yet no matter how the old bird hovered, with nose to mountain and tail to sky, the closeness of the front rotor to the mountainside forbade a front-door touchdown. Abruptly, it soared into the twilight sky and flew back to Durango – minus dog and handler. Hound and friends had to hike down into base.

A cold night would soon fill our high valley, and the handler – Les, a moose of a man with a vigorous voice – had no sleeping gear. Rescuers teased and laughed when I invited Les to share my two-man tent. Grateful for my offer, he said, "You don't have to worry about me, I'm almost sixty."

"Well, you don't have to worry about me either. We're the same age."

Supper, quick and savory, was cooked by rangers over a wood fire. Afterwards, in the grey darkness, Les and Babe, the dog, watched me crawl into the tent and lay out Larry's pad and fluff up a rescue team's extra down bag. Because my tent was pitched sideways on a slope, I lined up our four boots between us for a bundling-board. I would take the top side, and make an effort to keep from rolling down. Babe, told to sleep at the open flap, was tied to a thick log.

I confided to Les, "What I really want is your bloodhound."

"Yeah. She's two years old. Raised her myself."

In public, gruff and full of swear words to his hound, Les now bid her "goodnight" in a kind and gentle voice.

At daybreak, though night still lingered in the basin, we were awakened by a male voice singing "Oh, What a Beautiful Morning." I sat up and found the tent collapsed. One trip around by a hound and her log had buried two sleepers.

The rangers cooked bacon and eggs over an open fire. The bowls we ate from, submerged in tall grass, looked like tundra bird nests. Strange – everyone had broken down his tent and packed as though for departure that evening. Did we feel an instinctive urge, or was our behavior impulsive, without thought? I packed my gear that dawn because the positive phrase, "We'll find Larry today," was grooved inside my skull, playing constantly.

At the early briefing, base assigned eight search teams, each with two, three or four members, which were to be scattered at search areas on the mountain or in nearby basins – delivery by the flying workhorse. Les and Babe were Chinooked back to Durango, Les firmly covering Babe's ears with his hands to protect her hearing.

I've noticed that any search dog who travels in a Chinook with his trainer must have the patience to tolerate some ear protection. On a search mission to Mount Blanca, I had watched Ann, a young trainer, lift her Labrador's ear flaps to gently insert sponge ear plugs; this was followed by a winter scarf tied, peasant style, around the head. The dog looked sheepishly at the searchers watching and grinning, but accepted his eccentric hat. I suppose he was happy not to have to wear a seat belt.

Larry's backpack was carried to base and inventoried. His driver's license, train ticket back to Durango, and $72 were inside. He had to be on the mountain.

Mel would direct the two pilots in dangerous landings squeezed between formidable rock walls. Perhaps the most experienced member on the mountain, he sat in the tight commander's seat behind the pilots, shuffling four voluminous maps, each having a piece of Aeolus in a corner.

Mike, an experienced radio man, and I were to set up a radio relay on the remote 13,800-foot saddle-ridge between Aeolus and its brother, 14,039-foot North Aeolus. (The question of whether North Aeolus is a separate fourteener isn't settled yet. The airy saddle between their summits drops only slightly over 200 feet.) With us on the ridge, teams north of the mountain could relay messages through us to base, south of the mountain. Poor Mike, always stuck with me; Mike, of all people – he's quiet and I'm not.

I slung 200 feet of climbing rope across my shoulders in case the ridge should turn mean, and Mike carried the heavy radio. When we boarded the crowded aircraft I saw solemn eyes and unsmiling lips. The pilots flew tight circles in the basin to gain elevation. The basin is narrow, only three-quarters of a mile in width, and our landing zone was over 2,000 feet above. A corkscrew was the only way to fly. Mel motioned four times with his hands to Mike and me that we were the first team out the ramp. Either Mel was nervous or my face was blank.

The ship would hover only for seconds. When the crew chief raised his palms, I snatched my pack and rope, threw each over a shoulder and bounded to the ramp. Always slippery with oil, the ramp was now cranked to slope downward. At the ramp end was nothingness – we hovered eight feet in the air. Too late to prepare or to stop, I burst out, with my left hand on the ramp to ease the drop to an unknown landing. Oddly enough, the helmet, with my head inside, struck the firm ground first, then the hands, and last the knees – a five-point landing. I staggered to my feet and ran across the gravel shelf to crouch behind a boulder next to Mike while the 125 mph rotor blast departed. My dramatic exit had left me stunned and gasping. One year later I was talking with a rescuer from another group who had been on the flight; she told me that the ship had lurched up as I dropped off the ramp, flipping my feet over my head. Thank God for the helmet.

Our climb to the saddle was over narrow rock ledges fringed with alpine flowers. The cool air, containing significantly reduced oxygen compared to sea level, exploded like champagne in my lungs. In a moment Mike had his relay ready and sat waiting for customers. My eyes turned glassy to see the drop on the other side of the ridge. Haphazardly piled rocks, big as elk, formed a crude 400-foot wall that built up from under an immense snowfield lying in Ruby Creek basin below. Peak after peak over 13,000, with vertical walls of rock that rose from valley floor to summit, marched north to the skyline. Until comfortable with this aerie, I didn't dwell on our exposure.

With my back to the drop, I studied rough crags rising over 1,000 feet above a massive headwall of rock that encloses the lovely Chicago Basin. Some of these peaks have names, some only numbers – like Peak 11 or Peak 16. Others are ignored. Imagine being a peak 13,995 feet high and nobody bothering to number or name you! In Colorado you must rise over 14,000 feet to get attention. Some of the walls slope up straight as a pin, 2,000 feet from treeline to summit; others are carved with terraces, ledges and benches filled with snow melt – water that tumbles down to run away with the Colorado River.

I considered a rapid climb up the rocks to the North Aeolus summit – only 200 feet above – just to be able to say I'd climbed it. But our serious mission gave me perspective; for the first time, I pierced the crust around my ego and saw the conquering of a summit as ludicrous. Nobody conquers a mountain. Such conceit! In my sudden maturity I was content with a ridge.

While I was studying these ancient Rockies, two La Plata men had passed along our ridge and now stood on the summit. They radioed base that Larry's signature was not in the summit register. The register, a small note pad stuffed in a bottle or rusty can, is held down on a summit by rocks and often hidden from view. Yesterday, Outward Bound hadn't located the register – maybe Larry hadn't either. They noticed freshly torn pages from a Bible, one of which had blown down to the snowfield and had been picked up by Mel the day before. Van didn't know whether Larry had carried a Bible, although he considered Larry "very definitely" a religious person.

Later, when the afternoon sun beat down on our chilly perch, and peaks 125 miles away stood naked in the quiet air, and radio traffic eased, a drowsy solitude came over Mike and me. Our remoteness was shattered, however, when the calm message came to us for relay: "We have a body."

A La Plata team of two men, one on his first mission, had been searching talus slopes (a mass of rock fragments below a cliff) far from the normal ascent or descent routes, when "something didn't look right." Climbing higher, they found the body where it had fallen headfirst into large boulders. A walking stick lay in the rocks. The hair was grey. A red fanny pack was buckled around the waist. Elastic bandages encased both knees. Permission to lift out the body was requested from the Durango coroner, and when granted by radio at 1:30, the search was over.

Although I never did see Larry, I felt an affinity with this mountain climber near my age – a kinship, an understanding of what he loved, perhaps loved too much. With one hand on the shovel handle, he'd been traversing a skittish rock slope above a 500-foot drop. Whether he lost his balance or whether his boots caused a rock avalanche is unknown. Lacerated fingertips tell only of his struggle to save himself.

The Chinook flew over, lowered a litter, and hovered at 40 feet to make the body recovery. The site, at 13,000, was at an

elevation where oxygen in the air is in short supply. Thinking often blurs. In the ship, Captain Charlie made a sudden
lunge for the crew chief, hypoxic from low oxygen, who was
leaning over the open cargo hatch
while not clipped to the fuselage. The
bumpy hover could have pitched him
out the hatch. He had been sitting on
a bench or standing by the cargo
hatch, which doesn't require much effort. He had allowed his breathing
rate to slow down, reducing the oxygen entering his lungs and eventually
the oxygen concentration in his blood.

litter in use

This lack of oxygen is what high-altitude sickness is all about.
Symptoms – confusion, memory loss and forgetfulness –
show up right away. Worse symptoms – psychotic behavior,
hallucinations, disturbed gait or nerve paralysis – can follow.

The crew chief held a shepherd's hook in his hand to haul
in the litter, like freight. As the litter rose on the hoist,
Captain Charlie was shaken to see the body tied across, not
around, the waist. The six-foot litter must tip to enter the 4-by-
4 foot hatch; the body could slide out. The chief, now clipped
in, tugged the litter firmly against the fuselage's exterior for
the brief flight to base. "I don't like to do that," Captain
Charlie told me later. "Rescuers must tie around the neck, if
nothing more." The 25-pound litter, of tubular steel in an
open construction that encloses a person within its sides, is a
marvelous invention. Invaluable for live victims, it is also
useful for body recoveries where the only requirement is that
the body be soundly held on the litter. Webbing laces down
the arms and shoulders, the waist, the thighs and feet. Of
course, a body bag with handles doesn't need a litter.

During the afternoon the aircraft gathered scattered teams
alerted by our relay, while Mike and I watched a thunderhead
grow and darken in the eastern sky. I felt that sitting on an isolated alpine ridge with a metal radio was begging for a bolt. As
the storm drifted closer, base called: "Relay, all teams are in."
Time to leave.

"Why don't we hike down, Mike, and see the flowers?"

"It's two thousand feet, Peggy. Let's get the chopper
instead." He radioed the request to base.

We abandoned our precarious perch and danced a lively

step down to the landing zone just as hail and lightning and
thunder unleashed their rage. During the bursts, base called:
"Pilot says storm's bad. Walk down." My laughter, aimed at
Mike, uncorked the day's tension. When the storm clouds
scattered, our silent descent over the snowfield and through
the willows – two hours of unwinding – was a soothing balm
that helped to heal the loss of Larry.

10. HOAX

For reasons of their own, people sometimes stage their disappearance; however, search teams continue to hunt for any reported lost person, for our distrust may be invalid, our loss of interest a tragedy.

Pushing aside the drenched willow thickets, I peered around for the body of a missing woman. I was looking – yet afraid of finding. A moody cloud hanging low overhead dropped a furious lightning bolt that lit the swamp. A crash of thunder shook my courage in the eerie afternoon, while hail and rain pounded on my head. Alone, I wandered through a psychic's vision in slippery mud beside the stream. My seance with two psychics, a glass ball and unseen spirits had sent me into this swamp – a quest that was producing nothing but a spooked searcher.

The massive hunt in May, which ended in this macabre marsh, had begun days earlier in a motel room in Cañon City, a town 35 miles south of Colorado Springs, during an all-night discussion between a Wisconsin accountant and his problem-troubled wife. At dawn the 39-year-old woman drove away in their car and late that evening hadn't returned. The husband reported her missing before midnight, just as the vehicle was found abandoned – key in the ignition, traveler's checks and money intact on the seat – at the Pikes Peak toll gate, 50 miles north of Cañon City.

El Paso Search and Rescue was alerted. Although on the team only seven months, and never before in a massive search, I was given charge of the husband, with no directions as to what that entailed. He stood tall, thin, thoughtful; he was always appreciative and understanding of our search problems. Despite the great stress he was under, we developed a warm friendship, and he told me of their life together. I felt his wife was restless, somewhat unstable, and had simply gone away. People had seen her walking near the toll gate and some even had talked with her, while her husband waited for her return to Cañon City.

Early on the day she had left – before being reported missing by him and before newspapers and television could grab the story – she had requested a ride from engineers waiting at the unopened toll gate on the 19-mile road to the summit, but was refused. Our briefing mentioned, "The death of their infant son a half year earlier might stir in her a desire to communicate with him from the summit," but the husband discredited the importance of that to me. Nonetheless, when the car was discovered, two searchers rode the dark and deserted mountain road to the silent summit, where, at dawn, they searched for footprints unsuccessfully in the fresh snow.

The wife hadn't made it up the mountain, because during the first day several people had seen her walking slowly along wooded roads near Ute Pass, where earlier visitors – Ute Indians, buffalo and explorers – had passed through the narrow valley on the way to their South Park hunting grounds. Residents in the small villages in this pass (around 7,500 feet) below Pikes Peak are known by their neighbors. Even today a stranger walking the shaded trails and winding roads stands out like an albino bear.

She had asked a hiker, an 82-year-old woman, "Could you give me an old blanket? Some food and water? I want to sleep on the mountain. No, I'm not ill, but I've had an unpleasant experience."

When interviewed later, the old woman said, "She seemed calm and pleasant and most grateful for the blanket, the two thermoses and the sandwiches I gave her."

Once the wife was described as a missing person, her purse, wallet, coat and shoes were found alongside a small motel –

and people remembered her walking down a country road barefoot. The search for her began and gained momentum rapidly. In our briefing she was said to be, "wandering aimlessly, like a lost child, needing help." The husband, however, knew her as a smart woman, capable of walking away from a marriage.

While we sought her, I became fascinated with the dichotomy between our team's actions and the husband's words. The coordinators, reading their own interpretation into what he said, were off on the emotional charge of a major search. Aghast, I decided to cool down one of them by telling him privately of some information from the husband, facts that pointed strongly to a possible hoax. He listened a moment, then turned away from me. The search was his ego trip.

The hectic hunt continued with 50 volunteers from groups on the eastern slope – Pueblo Civil Defense, Teller, Alpine, Larimer, the Civil Air Patrol, Search and Rescue Dogs of Colorado and fire departments from Ute Pass. Excitement reached a crescendo when the blanket and two thermoses were found strung out like clues along a steep trail leading up to a rocky ridge. The next day her underwear and outer clothing were found in a bag discarded in a nearby meadow. All her clothes were now collected. The weather was too cool for nakedness, yet the public was convinced a woman was running bare through the woods.

At first I believed the wife had walked away from her marriage, but now these clues told me she had also baited us, leading searchers, and most importantly her husband, into this deception – her apparent death on the mountain. In an attempt to find her, the steep forest on Pikes Peak surrounding her vehicle and her clues was carefully probed, sometimes twice. A bloodhound and a German shepherd sniffed the road and trails for her scent. A Huey helicopter roamed up a high and wild valley, scaring a brown bear. A touch of hysteria crept into the pursuit when an imaginative young girl mistook a distant jogger in white running through a pine-clad foothill for the naked wife. Immediately the Huey and search teams stormed the hill like a scene from Vietnam.

At the end of the third day, George, one of our coordinators, stood by the dark toll gate and quietly told the husband, "We're closing the search down. We've followed up on everything."

"What am I to do? I can't abandon her!" was his lament.

During a search, or even after a mission is closed, psychics and mystics from near and far away relate their visions by letter and phone. Usually their descriptions are fat with gory details; others are loose and vague, and applicable to many sites. Mission leaders listen politely, then frequently ignore them. Rarely are reports checked out, because experience shows they usually never lead to a find. And the information is kept from field searchers, for it might influence their thorough searching. Inevitably, psychics want to help, to be involved in a mission and to test their supernatural abilities. On this mission, a request came in for $2,000 to $3,000 in exchange for information on the whereabouts of the victim. Rescuers were angry that anyone would hope to profit from the suffering of others.

After the search for the wife was closed down, a coordinator – the same one who didn't want to hear my information pointing to a possible hoax – told me to follow up on reports from mystics. Why not? I thought.

I was invited to a seance by two local psychics, a mother and son, to be held in a home close to where the wife had disappeared. Even before we began, I was stiff with nervousness. A real seance! Six of us gathered behind curtains to sit around a table on an afternoon bright with sunshine. The young man was of normal appearance, wearing neither horns nor halo. His mother, middle-aged and friendly, was an unassuming woman without airs. The crystal ball, carefully unwrapped from blue velvet, was laid on the table. The son explained the ball wasn't for viewing a scene or foretelling the future; instead it was for focusing his energies. I didn't want any cynical thoughts to destroy their trance, so I listened and believed.

With bowed head and closed eyes, the mother, speaking as the wife, and the son, as moderator, slipped into an intense trance. The mother's voice never faltered in its slight accent, an accent she didn't have in life. The other visitors listened, never moving or speaking. I jotted notes of her rapid and highly emotional delivery. She covered a wide range of subjects concerning the husband and his missing wife. Facts were brought up that could have been deduced from newspaper articles and photos taken during the search. Other information hadn't appeared in the media, but was known by coordinators and had been briefed to team members. Later I was dying to mention to the husband, the psychic's explicit discussion of personal details, but didn't think I should. And to this day I don't know if the details were correct.

The mother described in graphic terms the scene where the wife's body lay. Her vision spared no details. They emerged from the trance an hour later, glazed with sweat and blinking from the sudden light shining in their eyes. Their sincerity was obvious. After, I slogged through three swamps in Ute Pass and two stream beds along the toll road until all the possible sites in their visions had been checked, but to no avail.

On an eerie afternoon two days later, the young man and his mother unfolded another seance on a rotting table abandoned beside a dreary swamp. I hoped nobody driving on the highway high above us looked down and recognized me sitting by the crystal ball, and later emerging from the swamp, soaked and skittish.

The $2,000-to-$3,000 professional psychic, an Illinois woman, who had a friend in the area to feed her details, gave a coordinator her information – a description of the locale where the wife was raped and murdered. She even did it without money, when she saw that none was forthcoming. I searched possible sites, but without success. The husband remained in Ute Pass for several days to show her photo in the occasional restaurant, bar or motel in the area.

Today, five years later, the wife remains missing. Perhaps the greatest mystery is how, without clothes or money or friends, she vanished in a mountain village. Or has she really remained on the mountain, forever vanished from our sight? The husband and I reminisce by phone at least once a year. He now wishes to forget her. In fact, a judge has declared them divorced on a desertion basis, since death can't be assumed for seven years.

a pika hiding in the rocks

A cynic is an irritant in rescue work, for he smells the odor of deception in every clue. I discovered my skepticism mounting, justified or not, after the search for the missing woman on Pikes Peak.

Then, on a benign October evening five months later, a mission was called in response to what was obviously a fraud. Details were dubious. Regardless, somebody must go up and check out the summit. When I heard the words, "We'll drive to the top of Pikes Peak and search under winter conditions," I blurted out, "I'll go! Where do we meet?" My cyncism was promptly buried.

While grinding our way up the 19-mile toll road to the snow-drifted summit, our team chuckled over the mission details. Mike, our leader, said, "A man who refused to be identified called the newspaper to say he and his girlfriend rode the cog train to the summit today. He left her in the snow a quarter-mile down Barr Trail by the metal sign saying 'Golden Stairs' and rode back down."

The top quarter-mile of Barr Trail, just below the summit, isn't a summer stroll in two feet of snow. Skinny rock ledges disappear under the flakes, and one can easily get off the trail and onto the wrong ledge and end up staring down a 20-foot cliff. The trail itself is more an opening through treacherous rocks. We would be like blind men probing with our canes.

The man added grim details to his story – the smoking of pot, an argument, a blow. Since all passengers on the cog train that day had returned to the station and the toll road was closed to the public, we agreed that a hoax was probable. Still, the story required checking – even at midnight.

Mike and Kevin were to stay with a radio and the emergency gear at the summit house while two teams would scout in the snowcover for footprints and then later, turn back up. The first team, Dennis Kelly (a seasoned mountaineer) and Bill Hunt (an untried member), would search on the north ridge where wind had scoured the rocks of snow. The second team, Raven (a husky and forceful Air Force Academy officer), Max Urata (a silent member of Japanese extraction) and I would move down the trail, buried under flakes light as goose down. Our starlit night hardly required headlamps, but the trail, chiseled in steep cliffs, demanded the yellow circle to probe for switchbacks. When an ice axe struck buried trail rock, a metallic clang echoed across the snow. After an hour of scouting we reached the metal sign. Raven took a look around and called out, "This is a hoax. With this deep snow, we'd find some tracks left, even if a strong wind blew today." There had been no wind. The 12-degree air moved softly, almost imperceptibly, against our bare faces. A sense of peace and beauty settled around us.

Watching a moist, dense cloud gently wrap itself around the peak, we turned and followed our leg-holes back up to the summit house. Now cold stars in the sky and vivid lights in town were lost to our sight, replaced by falling snowflakes, big as apple-blossom petals in spring. I looked up to see that the summit-house light, a 100-watt bulb, now lit the falling flakes. I felt there was no place on earth I would rather be during this romantic night than at 14,000 on my beloved peak.

"Rescue twenty-eight?" Mike radioed Dennis. "We're ready to go back to the top. This is a fraud. What's your location?"

"I can't figure our location in this cloud. There's no visibility. We're still searching for the other team's prints in the snow."

We waited an hour – while Raven napped on the concrete floor and awakened severely nauseated from the hypoxia of insufficient oxygen in the blood. I had been tempted to warn him not to sleep at that elevation, to stay awake and to breathe deeply; but instead I minded my own business and walked around, staying on my feet. Nobody offered Raven oxygen from our tanks, and Raven was probably too embarrassed to request any.

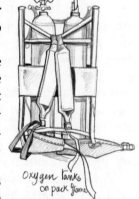

Dennis then called, "I've got the tracks. But Bill's faint, has a headache and is vomiting." Another rescuer out with hypoxia. This high-altitude sickness would keep Bill, a city-man, from ascending the 700 vertical feet to the top. We had a victim, finally.

"Max, put on the two oxygen tanks and go back down to Bill," Mike

Oxygen tanks on pack frame

directed. "Kevin, you go, too. Are you going, Peggy?"

"Well, I think I should." Don't let Mike think I'm tired, not even at 3:00 a.m.

With the trail already broken by our deep tracks through the snow, we made good time going down and soon saw two yellow lights bobbing below our cliff. Receiving oxygen from our tanks, a sheepish Bill hiked back up the trail to the summit house, which is better than being carried or dragged – especially by me.

With both teams back, we left the summit in our two rescue vehicles and traced the icy switchbacks 8,000 feet down the dark road, while speculating on the hoax. The others accepted the hospitable night on the summit and discussed the mission without bitterness, feeling that any mission is good training. But my own less than honorable thoughts dwelled on members who in the past were angry when they had been asked to leave the group. I wondered if one of them was capable of the deception.

In my time with the group, only two members had been asked to leave, and that was after considerable patience was shown. One was 21 years old, cocky, ready for a fight and unfairly critical of the efforts of other members. The other was dishonest. Some people have wanted to join but never made it into probationary status. A young man of 18 years was immature and defensive toward criticism. A fine rock climber in his 30s wasn't liked by the group, and he leered at the young women on the team.

Searches for these two women – one real but missing, the other imaginary – are not representative; indeed, they are rare instances. Even more infrequent is the hoax where we searchers have the last laugh. In fact, such joy has occurred only once. During this search of my first summer on the team, I was shuttling children to eastern colleges and unable to volunteer. Nevertheless, weird details rising from the hunt make an incredible story.

The search began modestly: a Fort Carson soldier had not returned from a canyon south of Pikes Peak. Since he was an avid survivalist, he was almost surely alive. Maybe take one day. When members in a Chinook peered down into Beaver Creek Gorge, just south of Pikes Peak, where he was reported missing – he and his rifle – questions and doubts ricocheted inside many heads. Dark-pink granite cliffs, formed a billion years ago from molten rock that pushed into the earth's crust, guarded a sinuous creek. Even the overbearing dirt slopes, speckled with piñon pine, gave off a sense of treachery. Might take more than a day.

Clues of the soldier's presence lay scattered near the canyon
mouth – a car, a backpack and clothes hung neatly on a fence.
An arrow pointing upstream beside his initials was scratched
in sandy dirt, soon followed by his dogtag. Mel, with two
members, probed up the gorge, crossing the creek like a
bootlace. He radioed base, "We've found a pair of tennis
shoes on a rock in the creek and a three-prong frog spear on a
grassy island. Now a carton of his brand of cigarettes in the
dirt. They're laid out. Easily seen by someone searching."
Then Mel's team came upon the soldier's .44 single-shot rifle
standing against a tree several miles up the gorge, a bullet
dropped over the barrel to keep rain out. Wondering if a
booby trap enclosed the gun, Mel stirred the surrounding
earth with a long stick. The search was no longer innocent – a
.44 makes a fair hole. From reading material and weapons
found in his quarters, coordinators also knew of the soldier's
deep interest in black martial arts.

"He's a model soldier. The Army's his life and love," his
commanding officer claimed. "He just reenlisted and got his
bonus. No, he wouldn't go AWOL."

But Chinook crews and tired searchers from throughout
Colorado, with raw and wrinkled feet inside soaked boots,
began to see clues as deceptions, planted perhaps to lead
authorities astray or to cause the "victim" to be declared dead.
After five days the search was closed and the gorge deserted;
speculation was the sole remnant of the enormous quest.

Half a year later the soldier, very much alive, was caught in
California during a burglary. Our revenge for the gorge pursuit was his arrest by authorities on AWOL charges. The evil
he inflicted on searchers came back in a circle to snatch him.

I was distressed by my absence during that search. To seek a
person, even an object, is an intriguing challenge, and I wail
within when I skip a mission. Not to mention the lure of
that secluded canyon and its inner gorge – where a mountain
lion leaves its sign; where a deer's brown eyes, a hawk's
sharp eyes observe a hiker; where dipper birds swim
underwater. Even without a search, I prowl that gorge in
every season.

The following February, however, the quest for a 26-year-
old West German citizen ended in cloudiness and conjecture.
To this day, it's a search unsolved and is likely to remain a

puzzle forever. The Himalayan-experienced skier, Reudi, was dropped by a friend at the highway that crosses 10,285-foot Cameron Pass, 50 miles west of Fort Collins and on the way to Steamboat Springs. Reudi planned to ski alone over gentle Thunder Pass in the Never Summer Range (which stretches along the Continental Divide) and into the west side of Rocky Mountain National Park. On the fourth day he would ski out and hitchhike back to his friend in Fort Collins. The plan was proper for a well-equipped expert. The trouble was, Reudi never appeared after the trek.

When his friend reported him missing, a full search was begun by the park service and Larimer County Search and Rescue. The next day, when our large team flew up in a Chinook, I gasped to see shoulder-high snow lying like whipped cream over gentle slopes that peaked a few feet below 13,000. Base buzzed with snowmobiles and searchers, some eating pancakes. Mosquitolike helicopters zipped out and back. Although still inexperienced, a member only a year, I was named a team leader – and from then on everything went haywire for me. In just two search days, how could so much go wrong? The mission was my nightmare.

At our landing zone the first day, I tossed my tent, sleeping bag and pad under a tree to lighten my load – having been assured of our return before nightfall. Of course, we never came back. At our team's destination, Lulu City, a chicken-feather sleeping bag was flown to me by chopper; because it turned out to be huge, our team dumped dozens of sandwiches, oranges and apples inside for my body warmth during a freezing night. I added my boots, radio, water canteen and myself. Lulu City isn't a city. Today it is abandoned, a wide spot along a stream enclosed by aspen. In 1880 this mining town held gold-ore dreams which proved false, and the disappointed miners drifted away. I lay in my bag under the stars and over four feet of snow with only a jacket and backpack for insulation. The next morning the strap on my five-foot-long Alaskan snowshoes broke, and I trudged the long way uphill to the landing zone with nylon string as a binding, while the clumsy sleeping bag on my backpack switched from side to side. After the day-and-a-half effort we had discovered nothing – except that I had crushed the sandwiches.

But another team, searching at Box Canyon, where Reudi's food cache, minus one meal, had been found prominently hung, came upon a snow cave. His backpack, stove, sleeping bag, tent and pad lay inside. His warm clothing, alpine skis and poles were missing, as was Reudi himself.

"You don't suppose he did all this and took off," I overheard a park ranger say. "It's all so perfect."

What Reudi might gain by being presumed perished was a new life in America. By skiing south along the Colorado River, here a thready stream, he could reach Trail Ridge Road, only four miles from his snow cave.

Teams weren't being gullible by pushing the search for five days – perhaps clues were authentic, nobody knew. Aircraft and skiers investigated nearby Mount Richthofen and Box Canyon. Men drove probes into avalanche debris. Teams spread out over wide snow slopes and narrow drainages.

When the warmth of summer melted the snow layers and avalanche deposits, rangers in helicopters and fixed-wing aircraft cruised low over the slopes, ridges and gulches. Other rangers ground-searched for countless days (the last thing rangers want is a dead body lying in the park). Larimer County Rescue ferreted out the area once again. Neither his body or bones, clothes or skis or poles, were ever found.

If Reudi took off, as I suspect he did, I should have felt bitterness toward him. But none surfaced. Instead I was preoccupied with a black cloud of shame that settled over my spirit whenever I recalled the errors I made as a team leader in the mission. Since then other missions have come and gone and I have grown a bit more experienced.

After the two missing women on Pikes Peak, the soldier in Beaver Creek Gorge and the German skier in Rocky Mountain National Park, a mission surfaced where the coordinator, Rich, admitted a hoax was suspected. By now, I was three years a member and knew we would go out, regardless of suspicions.

pager

When the pager on my belt issued the request for members, I gazed out the window and saw a brisk, snowy night in October. Might be fun. Appealing missions erupt in the hush of evening, when the wrap of darkness hides reality and prevents distraction, and when the spell of the night lends magic to a quiet search scene. This spell goes deep and entices searchers into the field even when a deception is suspected and sleeping hours are lost.

Rich told me to report to the Air Force Academy fire station. A deer hunter had reported to a rancher living in the valley just south of the Academy grounds that he had seen two cadets fighting their way out of the mountains through deep snow while hauling an injured buddy. The tale sounded fictitious because the hunter, the "reporting party," had disappeared to his home immediately.

By the time our team got there, the Air Force had already flown two search aircraft, Fort Carson had sent two MAST helicopters, and television's News Center 4 had cruised the area. Teams were assigned to both sides of the Academy's south boundary, where foothills, white from a recent blizzard, sneak up on the Rampart Range, lying west of the plains.

Our team of three – Mel, Annie and myself – began our hill search at 10:00 that night, with Mel saying, "These guys aren't here, what do you bet? But we have to give it a try."

For hours we plodded like refugees through crusted snow almost too deep to hike through, yet too shallow for snowshoes. Thick, wet clouds hung heavily just over our heads and over the distant city lights, giving off a romantic reflection that allowed us to turn off our headlamps with their stark circle of light and view the hills as crumpled cloth woven of black pine needles and white snow. We didn't speak, for fear the cadets would cry out and not be heard.

Hours later, in the deep of night, our hill blended with a higher ridge. I dropped my pack and snowshoes and said, "This is it. I climb no further. I know that buzzard told a lie." Annie agreed and sat quietly with me on the crusted snow. But Mel, alone and without a headlamp, chased the hoax across higher slopes for another hour. Meanwhile, silence emptied my skull and I felt an exquisite aloneness in the misty night.

We saw or heard no one, and finally departed just before dawn via another hilltop. Annie remarked, "Nobody would say at ten o'clock some chilly evening, 'Let's go out and hike through the mountains for six hours,' yet we were asked to do this and we've had a good time."

"It's all right to be peculiar if you know you're peculiar," I added.

And Mel finished with, "And we do!"

This mission, based on an illusion, was dredged out of an exhausted hunter's brain, but to us the search was not pointless; we found a reward in the night's effort.

At dawn the pursuit started again with fresh people – except Mel, who stayed over for another search attempt. During the afternoon, sheriff's deputies, following up on leads, uncovered the hoax. The 24-year-old hunter admitted telling the story to a rancher when he was cold, tired and wet and needed sympathy to get a ride to his car. He got the ride, went back for his deer lying on the snow, then drove home. The rancher called authorities and the intense search was on.

After the search was closed the costs were impressive. The Air Force provided over 500 man-hours for $10,000; rented two search aircraft for $288, two hours total; and provided delicious box lunches for our teams at a cost of $311.

The Army at Fort Carson supplied two MAST Huey helicopters which flew three hours at $264 per hour, making a total of $792. Fifty man-hours at $12 per hour make $600.

News Center 4 used their chopper for searching three hours, a total cost of $1,200.

Our El Paso team put in 312 man (and woman) hours at an equivalent cost of $8 per hour – if we had been paid, but, of course, we weren't – for a total of $2,496. Our rescue vehicle drank $50 in fuel.

The total came to $15,735 for this relatively simple search that lasted only 26 hours. The Air Force bill and Army costs were picked up by the government. But pilots must fly for practice, and military manpower is receiving pay, regardless. The news chopper was getting a story. We are volunteers, our fuel paid by cash donations. The total bill isn't as bad as it looks.

For giving out this false report to authorities, the hunter was charged with a misdemeanor. In two court visits and with the aid of a lawyer, he was released from charges, because he related his story to the rancher, not to authorities. The innocent rancher carried the hoax to authorities.

All these hoaxes, true or suspected, left me a cynic on later searchers – subject guilty until proven innocent. Nonetheless, if a Chinook ride is thrown in, if the terrain is mountainous, and if my adrenaline rises to meet the challenge, I'll race to the helicopter and take what comes, authentic or fraudulent.

11. RAPTURE

*Rapture is a euphoric trance which overwhelms
solo hikers and skiers who are deeply moved by a
summit view or snow conditions. Even rescuers are
susceptible to this ecstasy.*

Like the golden eagle probing across a cliff for a tasty ground squirrel, our Chinook hunted up a ragged ridge for the missing hiker. Upon reaching 12,600 feet, the aircraft hovered over bumpy, green tundra before slowly squatting and lowering its ramp. Ten of us rescuers dashed down the ramp and into the rotor wash to run and crouch behind jutting boulders. When the ramp clamped shut, the chopper roared into full power and lumbered into the evening sky.

The thunderous din was gone and the stillness of an alpine night descended upon our narrow perch on Mount Harvard, a masterpiece of a mountain in the Collegiate Peaks of the Sawatch Range, west of Buena Vista. Ancient glaciers high on Harvard's shoulders plucked rocks and sand from its walls, leaving cirques and U-shaped valleys. Torrential streams during the ice age dumped the debris over the Arkansas Valley floor. Although a walk-up, Harvard and its massive ridges – broken by rugged rock outcroppings that sweep assuredly up from the forest floor – make a peak that projects virility and strength. My eye traced our ridge to the 14,420-foot summit, bathed in yellow reflection from a summer sun already set.

At morning's first light the Chinook passengers – eight men from the sheriff's patrol of Buena Vista, plus Rich, an electrical engineer and a good companion on a mission, and myself from El Paso County – were to search that ridge for Mitch, a missing Louisiana lad. Yesterday the 17-year-old and his father had been on a one-day climb of Mount Harvard. At one point Mitch raced ahead. Later, his father couldn't find the youth on the summit, or anywhere on the way back, or at the trailhead.

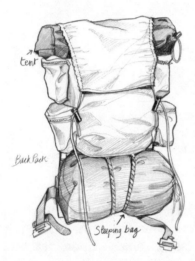

tent

Back Pack

Sleeping bag

By then he had been missing 28 hours. Even though the weather was fine, and he was backpacking a tent, sleeping bag and candy bars, I knew the dangers. "Maybe this search is a hysterical reaction, but someone must look, and it had better be a mountaineer," I told Rich. Harvard's ridges leading to the summit inspire fear as well as reverence. To a climber ascending, the route looks steep, cragged – the scale grand, overwhelming.

After the Chinook had left, we broke into three groups and were searching in the dusk, when radios brought startling news from a rescue team in the valley below our ridge. "We've got Mitch. He's uninjured. We're starting down with him now." When found he had been setting up his tent near Uncle John's cabin, a historic landmark along the well-traveled Pine Creek trail, for his second night. If he had been disoriented, one of the climbers headed for Harvard's summit could have pointed down the trail to the road. We wondered, silently, why he hadn't walked out. The 10 of us should have been irate, but we said nothing. I never saw him or learned his excuse for the odd behavior, but I surmise that Mitch fell into a rapture beyond his control when he stood alone on Harvard's dizzy pinnacle and gazed at the abundance of 14,000-foot summits stretching to the edge of the earth. Reduced oxygen at that high eleva-

tion added to his euphoria. Free of reality, he forgot his father
and hiked down a different ridge, to camp in the lovely
alpine valley so different from his Louisiana home.

During my lifetime I too have done some wandering –
actually more a form of absentmindedness which started in
kindergarten, when I sometimes forgot to walk directly
home; instead, I would explore in the opposite direction. My
forgetfulness didn't fade as I grew up. Today I find it appearing in rescue work, where I might, in my hurry, forget the
radio or the climbing gear.

But absentmindedness, where one is unaware of one's surroundings or duties, isn't the same as rapture. Rapture is
bliss, an ecstatic delight, where one is carried to another plane
of existence. I suspect that many suffer from this fascinating
syndrome, which is aided by a lack of oxygen and can be common in the mountains. Middle-aged trekkers in Nepal who
go for the high passes around 17,000 feet are said to get a little
crazy. Around Pikes Peak I take fascinating notes from my observations of flowers and wildlife around 13,000 feet; but at
home that night, 7,000 feet lower, the written thoughts are dis-
appointingly mundane. This joy and contentment fades
when one drops to the reality and oxygen of lower elevations.

I was relieved when they cancelled the search for Mitch.
But listening to the radio discussions among the three teams,
I began to realize, to my dismay, that we were climbing down
immediately. "Ask them to sleep now and hike out in daylight," I suggested to Rich.

They ignored the request and continued their rendezvous
plans over the radio. "Don't forget the old lady!" Could they
mean me?

Rich, the darling, corrected them, "She's not an old lady;
she's a spring chicken."

When gathered together we started for the valley, 2,000 feet
below, in starlit darkness that began to intrigue me.

"A trail crosses our ridge somewhere, but we don't know
where. Let's go down over the side," one of the men suggested.

"Straight down this abyss, Rich?" I was quivering.

"This is their turf, Peggy, so we'll follow."

The 10 of us bunched together at the first of many rock
slides. The rocks had crashed from higher cliffs and were
loose and big as mountain goats; but worst of all, when

stepped on, they and their neighbors began an unnerving slide downslope, avalanche-fashion.

My headlamp malfunctioned – or, rather, I malfunctioned, for in the dark I had installed two of the four batteries backwards, causing me to see with twilight vision the rest of the night.

After tense scrambling for over an hour I paused to rest, and heard only Rich and one other man nearby. Everyone else had veered off, lightning bugs on distant rock slides. I was puzzled. Rescue teams never scatter when returning from a mission, especially at night. Then I understood. "Rich, these fellows with us aren't searchers, they're elk hunters. Look at them, stalking alone, so their companion's boot won't snap a twig and scare an elk."

The rock slides ceased when we got down to treeline, and we struggled through thick aspen, tripping over fallen trunks. I wrestled with spruce limbs stronger than my own. I began to delight in the crazy night. Sometimes the greatest experiences come from a decision not one's own and not one's wish.

At midnight we came upon the wide valley trail along Pine Creek. "Just five miles to waiting cars!" came a shout.

When the ghostly trek was over and car lights shone through the trees, I finally straightened my back and stopped weaving from side to side. I was totally exhausted. "What a beautiful hike! Why did you fellows go so fast?" I said, not wanting the drivers or sheriff's patrol to think Rich and I, the last ones down, were totally wiped out.

Long after the mission I thought about Mitch and his rapture, and blushed to recall a late June search in my first rescue summer when a canyon of rare beauty in Rocky Mountain National Park stole my mind.

The theft began when a brief but severe June storm crashed into Flattop Mountain, which rises above Emerald Lake, and, together with Hallett Peak, reflects in the limpid jewel. The deluge drenched the few hikers caught on the trail. One was a husky 12-year-old boy, Robert, who had dashed ahead of his parents in his eagerness to reach the 12,326-foot summit. Behind him, his father followed slowly, searching for him unsuccessfully.

During the week a massive quest for Robert fanned out to take in hundreds of searchers, some tracking dogs and two helicopters. After an early morning briefing, a Fort Carson Chinook lifted a flock of us to the rounded summit of Flattop, where we clustered in teams against blustery wind from an angry sky.

"Fellows, our team leader is a woman ranger!" I boasted to my three male teammates. Women are scarce in rescue work; in my eight months on the team, I hadn't seen many. I soon learned, to my surprise, that she was not a smiler, she ordered rather than asked, and she was suspicious of me and my ability. Feeling defensive, I tried to slip into our brief conversations my countless climbs on California's Sierra peaks decades before her umbilical cord was severed, but never found the right moment.

"Come down, Parr. We'll join the others scattered below," she called to me in midmorning after an hour of searching along the gently sloping ridge below thumblike Hallett Peak. The weather was lowering, a misty day, and still winter at 12,000 feet, making us feel more remote in the park than we actually were. The scene was lifeless and bleak except for tiny fairy primrose blossoms pushing up between stones. The scale of remnant snowfields dwarfed the hardy primroses and our hunched figures. Distracted by snow buttercups that crowded on the edge of the lingering snowdrifts and tenuous mountain summits that crashed through my senses, I withdrew into a world of my own. I forgot her words.

Continuing to search on the ridge, I discovered a canyon of jumbled cliffs that dropped sharply below my boots – Chaos Canyon, according to my map. Spires and sculptures of rock rose for 1,000 feet into the sky, rich with rust, orange, mustard and lemon. Its volcanic beauty seized me, possessed me. I stood at the edge far too long, hidden by rocks, utterly enraptured – the search for Robert forgotten.

Suddenly I heard a footfall behind me. "Are you Peggy?" He knew my name?

Then I recognized him as a searcher from the Rocky Mountain Rescue team. "Your leader has been on the radio looking for you over an hour. And is she mad!"

When I rejoined our team she sat against a rock and lectured me with choice words. "My butt has been royally chewed out because I lost a team member. I told you to re-group, but you had to wander off."

While she growled on, I stood meekly before her like a naughty child. Inside, an inferno burned. I tolerate scolding from a man but never from another woman, a holdover from more than half a century ago, when I was an impressionable youngster – when cars had running boards and a boy on a bicycle lit street lamps with a taper and women and children did as men told them to do. Of course, she was right. But I was addled when I disappeared.

I survived that mission, but young Robert did not. After eight days and no sign of him, the futile search was closed. But six days later, hikers found his blood-stained sun visor. By then, snow crystals melting under a July sun had released Robert's body; climbers found it lying on snow and rock in the lower gully.

When the downpour began, he had hunted for a short-cut off the mountain. His fascination for the park's small glaciers enticed him into a fatal slide down an 800-foot snow gully. Held in wet snow high up between rock walls jutting out from the gully, his body was invisible to search teams. The lower half lay buried in snow while the upper half burned black from intense sun reflection.

If overpowering ·bliss chained Mitch to Harvard Mountain and me to Chaos Canyon, then our rescue team should be seeing more hikers under the same spell. I didn't wait long.

In January, Chris, an experienced 26-year-old cross-country skier from Steamboat Springs, was dropped off at Rabbit Ears Pass, in the Park Range, for an overnighter through high forest to the Mount Werner ski area – usually a one-day trek. He went solo. To ski in the back country without a companion is dangerous but never lonely. Moguls, groomed slopes and snowbunnies are replaced by deep powder, elegant glides and silence. He ignored the chance of a sprained ankle or an avalanche to gain valued isolation in a wilderness away from ski lifts.

Where the Continental Divide crosses the road at the pass, much of the terrain rises and falls gently and, when buried under heavy winter snowfalls, makes great cross-country skiing. However, there are steep areas that flow down between trees on the mountainsides, in the gullies and bowls and on the treeless slopes, that give birth to avalanches. Newly fallen snow lies over the firm crust of earlier snowfalls, but the fresh crystals won't bond to the old crust. When triggered by a pair of skis cutting across the slope, this unstable snow runs downslope with astonishing force, taking the skier with it. Slabs of snow laid down by wind over a weak layer of snow crystals can release, with the weight of a back-country skier, becoming a killer slide. A lone skier cannot shovel

Snow shovel

himself out. In 30 minutes a buried skier's chance of survival is half gone. It gives one pause.

Chris was well-prepared, with tent, sleeping bag, pad, food and compass. After he left, the roommate discovered Chris had forgotten his trail map. When he failed to show the next evening as a waiter in a local restaurant, the sheriff launched a search.

"Something's wrong. Should be easy to find him, though," searchers said. "His route is known." But three feet of snow-flakes from a storm the second day had buried his ski pole holes and the deep trench from his touring skis that other-wise would have led searchers to him. Steamboat's rescue team snapped their boots into three-pin bindings on skinny skis and glided north of the pass. They straddled snowmobile seats to charge back and forth, checking his route and attrac-tions along the way, almost drowning in six feet of snow. Turning off their engines, they listened for his voice.

On the second search day, our El Paso team of six flew from Colorado Springs to Steamboat inside a chilly Chinook with one window missing. The team was young and clowned in pantomime during the long, noisy flight. As team leader I had to manage some dignity before the flight crew, so could not join in. Also, I felt distracted by the deepening snow below my helicopter window. I had been a member less than two years, and a field leader for only one, so I was aware of soft spots in my head from inexperience.

We rode in four-wheel-drive pickups to 9,426-foot Rabbit

Ears Pass, following a snowplow slice into a six-foot-high white cake frosted with blue sky. At the pass I climbed on top of the cake and gazed across drifts of spruce trees submerged in a tidal wave of snow. Here the Divide looked like benign search country. Open meadows drifted like white islands through a tidy, green forest. This pass had a more friendly appeal than the stark and menacing tundra saddles along the Continental Divide in southern Colorado. "Yesterday I roared ninety miles through these flakes," said a driver, waving his hand across the wintry meadows.

Just when my team was preparing to search outlying areas, I caught the radio message, "He's just been seen walking into town!" Our missing skier? Impossible! Where has he been for two days? Did he limp? Why isn't he injured? No, I mustn't think that.

Before Chinooking back to Colorado Springs I glanced into search base window and read the mission leader's unamused face while he stood and questioned the young man, who sat in a chair munching a Big Mac. Later, answers leaked through the closed door when a Steamboat member filled us in. The missing map hadn't bothered Chris the first day. He came upon a snowmobile track striking north along the Continental Divide and skied over its packed surface. The heavy snowfall that moved in smothered that trail, but his compass would have told him the bearing west to the ski slopes of Mount Werner and to Steamboat.

Compass

I think Chris forgot his promise to return to the restaurant – who cares if the soup is cold? – because he skied north, lured by his Lorilei. I believe his actions shore up my theory of the frequency and power of euphoric moods brought on by lofty elevations and the deep powder of the high country. Found in below-zero air that numbs the face. Found in solitude. Found on skis hissing past white gnomes – spruce branches gracefully bent over and submerged under a foot of virgin flakes. I feel this rapture urged Chris north along the Divide for two days until his food was gone and hunger jolted him back to reality. Only then did he point the ski tips west for a five-mile-run down Soda Creek Canyon, where he nonchalantly emerged on the road for a three-mile hike into Steamboat Springs to face the penetrating stare of a mission leader.

12. SOLO

Mountains are dangerous and man is vulnerable.
When the rule against solo climbing is broken,
the mountain exacts its tribute.

"C'mon to the hot pool." Annie tossed this challenge over her shoulder through the chill October darkness.

"Hot pool?" In this remote backwoods corner? We had just emerged from a mission critique in a primitive lodge in the San Miguel mountains of the San Juan Range.

"Come and see." Her warm laughter hinted of a naughtiness that aroused my interest despite the late hour.

"I've no bathing suit or towel," I reminded Annie.

Her eyes taunted my naivete and mystified me. I'd visit the pool, but a dip was impossible. Who would ever pack a swimsuit on a search mission at El Diente Peak in southwestern Colorado? Strange.

We crunched over the frozen meadow and stepped into an empty shack that leaned away under a sagging roof. Inside, a fire exploded on the raised hearth, giving out intense heat, its sparks lying like rubies on the dusty wood floor. Neat bundles of clothing burdened benches along the walls, while a bare light dangled on a frayed cord from the tin roof.

A mumble of men's voices and a drift of steam emerged from a narrow door. Walking across the room, I peeked through the vapor at a dozen men standing to their shoulders in gravy-colored water bubbling from the earth into a rock-lined pool. In weak light from a blue bulb, I recognized my rescue friends. What a temptation! If only I had a suit.

I turned to face Annie and gasped to see her naked as a newborn.

She grinned. "Peggy, you'll love it" Then she disappeared through the vapors and screamed when she plunged into the hot water. The men roared with laughter. I stood before the fire, alone. Did I dare? What would my husband say? Worse still, what would the men say? But I deserved a hot soaking. Scouting through knee-deep snow for the missing climber had been brutal on my leg muscles. Then why tell my husband? Why hold back?

After stripping off my rescue clothing – except for old-lady panties – I leaped quickly into the water amid shouts of approval. Some rescuers were leaning against the rock rim, beards submerged, eyes closed, smiling to themselves. Snatches of mission stories drifted by. Hairy bodies began wandering through the water, laughing and howling like coyotes. Soon my Victorian modesty faded. I whipped off the panties and flung them across the pool where they splashed against the wall. More approval.

After a euphoric hour, several fellows and I ran screaming into the frosted night across powdery snow – each footprint an agony – and slid into a small shallow hot pool. In time the men leaped out, rolled their naked bodies over the snow while uttering barbaric noises, and dashed inside. I sat alone in the foot-deep water, my hair quick-frozen, and gazed up Dolores Valley to El Diente – 4,000 feet of silver glistening in the moonlight.

These men and we two women had come to isolated Dunton, a tiny community boasting this lodge of logs ravaged by sunshine and storms, to search for a missing peak-bagger (a mountain-summit collector) on the 14,159-foot forbidding mountain that dominated the valley. El Diente is a pinnacle rising like a gigantic snaggletooth 1,000 feet into the sky from a steep and long jaw ridge.

The hunt for Bill, a 35-year-old engineer, who wanted "one more fourteener before winter set in," was already in its fifth day when we arrived. Any mountain in Colorado 14,000 feet and over is a fourteener, and there are at least 54 of them.

"I'm climbing the peak on Saturday. If I don't get back by Sunday noon, call the sheriff," he had cautioned his wife.

When Bill didn't appear by Sunday noon, she talked to the sheriff, who soothed her. In Colorado only the county sheriff can initiate a search, and this was done on Monday.

Despite its being midweek, when rescue team members find leaving jobs somewhat chancy, 10 of our El Paso people shook themselves loose for the mission 400 miles down the road in the San Juan Range. To my relief, at dawn the Air Force swept the eastern slope volunteers into a C-130 and flew us over the Continental Divide to Durango, where a retired school bus without springs bounced us up the Dolores Valley to Dunton on a road full of potholes. A pickup loaded us for the run to base, a small grassy meadow along Dolores Creek surrounded by a fir and aspen forest.

huey helicopter.

The mission's logistics officer, Zach Hargraves, a bony and stern member of La Plata Search and Rescue, with the observant eyes of a marmot, stood beside base (an ancient bus painted brilliant orange and parked in the meadow) and lamented during our briefing, "He went alone on an unknown route to this summit, which demands plenty of experience. On Monday, United Search and Rescue from Cortez searched over bare ground. Then Captain Charlie flew down on Tuesday in a Fort Carson Huey helicopter and cruised the lower ledges of the ridge. But, remember, the little Huey – even with only two on board – has a ceiling around 12,600 feet. We still need coverage of the upper 1,400 feet, from the Huey's ceiling to the summit. Tuesday night the first winter storm hit El

Diente's slopes and dropped three feet of snow. Wednesday night we asked for volunteeers from other teams. Now Thursday noon, here you are."

People in a parked four-wheel-drive riveted their eyes on us during our equipment shuffling – changing gear from a backpack to a daypack – on a canvas tarp laid over powdered snow and shriveled wildflowers.

"Zach, who are they?" I wondered.

"The family. Drove non-stop from Minnesota."

When we were ready, the chopper, buzzing back and forth delivering teams like a blue jay storing seeds, flew into base and wedged itself down between trees, bus, creek, fire and rescuers. The rotor and its whirling knives made a windy insanity out of the tight scene.

Our team's search area was the slope below the south jaw ridge, just at tree line, and the pilots hovered close to the loose snow for an easy jump. In the Huey, "first in" means last out – often my fate. I leaped from the unsteady machine and ran through a blizzard kicked up by the blades to my teammates already huddled in the snow. The racket and wind didn't diminish, so I lifted my head to study the helicopter through finger slits and noticed the co-pilot staring at me and jerking his thumb toward the open rear door. I dashed back and slammed the heavy door for the tender pilots.

We kicked through the fluffy flakes, not needing snowshoes, each team member searching in a loose line for the missing climber. The Tuesday-night tempest had thrown a white blanket over fresh footprints, discarded clothing or food wrappers. Before long I  was stepping on rock humps, stamping through grass clumps, and scraping fallen logs with my boots. The thought occurred to me, we could be walking over Bill's body and not know it; every bulge in the snow begged for examination.

The dry, cold air of early winter cut our throats and cancelled my sleepiness from the pre-dawn departure. At the head of our valley, a stream drained an immense higher basin which in summer crashed noisily from an overhanging cliff; but during the frozen nights of autumn, the stream gradually gave birth to delicate, milky icicles which lengthened and fattened from dribbling water until they hung with grace and threat, not touching the ice pool below, to over 100 feet. Thousands of feet of white mountainsides soared above to wall in this treeless alpine basin which, though not frightening, was on such a grand scale that the scene burned into my brain, to be relighted months later for reflection.

When the day was closing down the helicopter pilots gave us a lift to base, where pickups continued the journey to Dunton for the night. After the imposing alpine basin below El Diente, I felt numb to new impacts until a tranquil moment occurred during a raucous dinner when I looked about and saw Dunton as a gift from the nearby forest.

Wood shakes on the roof, hand-split back in the 1890s, kept rain off the lodge, whose walls were crude-sawn planks of Engelmann spruce. Subalpine fir from tree line crackled in a fireplace laid up of creek rocks dragged in behind horses long dead. Elk, a delicacy, was served from recent inhabitants. And backwoodsmen, their beards dense as eagle nests, sat at the bar, their laughter rich from local whiskey. The line where earth ended and lodge began blurred that night.

The family, their faces solemn, sat with Hunter Holloway, the mission leader and a fatherly man filled with compassion and tact. They took no notice of the festivities. Their grief was visible, giving me guilt over my happiness.

At the evening critique, Zach called out to the crowd of rescuers, "Today a new 'last-seen point' was reported by hikers, who say they talked with Bill Saturday morning near the north ascent route to the summit." This vital information pinpointed Bill's route. A "last-seen point" is the focal point on which a search is based.

Eight teams tramped the next morning, one to the snowed-in summit. I was a team leader for five rescuers, including a 14-year-old mature youth from a Denver group that takes young ones. He wasn't the first I had seen of the Arapahoe Rescue Patrol, made up of high school students from Littleton. Those with whom I've worked have been well-trained and in control of their enthusiasms.

My search area was a drag: only 10,000-foot elevation, boring without a view, and not on Bill's route. The snow was becoming wet and heavy as concrete, and my leg muscles knew. To make matters worse, base handed me my search map showing their orange bus marked in a wrong location, which confused and irritated me.

While studying the map with a young airman on our team, I moaned, "Here I'm the team leader and you're reading the map better than I am."

"You can be the queen, Peggy, and I'll be your prime minister," was his sly reply.

I listened over my radio to transmissions from teams searching at higher elevations, feeling vicarious excitement. Suddenly a message from Fort Carson's commanding general was passed to Captain Charlie, ordering him to fly the machine back, "You're exceeding the Huey's flying time without a major overhaul." I wasn't privileged to hear Captain Charlie's comment when he received the message in the Huey. Knowing his gift for words, I'm sure it was unrepeatable.

We struggled up a steep hill intending to scout two small lakes hidden in snowflakes and spruce branches. When the snow level crept higher up my thighs, futility and tiredness set in; at 11,000 feet, my thinking was becoming affected by the reduced oxygen. Since the team was without snowshoes, I decided to skip the second lake. I felt Bill would never have gone that far off course. As we approached the lower elevation on our return, my conscience thawed, guilt appeared, and I realized Zach might suspect my devious decision.

"Sit down on these rocks, fellows, we don't want to return before the sun sets," I told the team. Zach would wonder why we didn't take longer.

At base we entered the old bus together and flopped down on metal seats. Why didn't the young men go out by the fire? With the entire team listening, Zach proceeded to question me on the area covered.

"Did you look across the trails, go up the slopes, check out each lake?"

His voice was sharp with precision, and I slumped in my seat, eyes studying the floor, answering, "Yes, yes, yes ... "

When the inquisition was over I was wet with sweat. Why did I lie about the second lake, when I hold the truth so high? Rescuers have large egos and strain to appear without fault. Why was I afraid to be less than perfect? Why must I hide my slip in judgment? Why didn't I just say, "Hell, no, we didn't do the second lake"? Perhaps I was afraid of his words. He couldn't kill me; I was a volunteer. I never found out what the team thought of my deception. My mistake returns to me often – as a lesson.

Six nights and a snowstorm had tolled the bells for Bill. At the critique that night we heard sad words for the family now in Cortez: The search is suspended until spring melt. A C-130 will come to Durango tomorrow morning for you eastern slope folks." Unfortunately, an incomplete search never releases its grip on a rescuer.

In the weak light of dawn and when only half dressed, I heard a faint rotor purr. Sounded like the Huey, which had flown back to Fort Carson. Strange how the mind works. When the purr strengthened and settled down next to the lodge, I couldn't deny anymore the little Huey and its master, Captain Charlie. We speculated on what he told the commanding general.

The two pilots didn't shut down while Tom and another engineer, both working under contract for the Department of Energy and who had detected heat activity during the previous Eagle Peak Mission at the Air Force Academy, stepped out carrying an infrared instrument. The remarkable black box, costing $60,000 and looking like a small hand-held TV, is a tool in a mission – like dogs, searchers and helicopters – and, as can be imagined, is least effective where deer and rabbits are abundant. The mountain is coldest, and heat contrast from a live or dead body greatest, 30 minutes before dawn. Now was after dawn, but they would try. A coordinator hopped into the helicopter with the pilots, Captain Charlie and the three men, and all flew up to El Diente.

Before most of us had finished breakfast, Zach charged into the room and stood with a dazed expression.

"Charlie just called to say they have your hiker."

We put down our forks and cups and stared at him. The body, lying at the 12,200-foot level and 2,000 feet below the summit, had evidentally fallen from a rock rib and dropped a considerable distance. The Huey descended to Dunton, where we greeted them with awe. "We were lucky," Tom said softly.

Captain Charlie explained that many sweeps across the north face indicated a hot spot. When the Huey made passes close to it, with the chopper flicking sparks off rocks with its blades, the rotor winds blew snow off Bill's shoulder, exposing his bright-orange hunter's vest. A search team ascending the north side had been close on Thursday, but the body was invisible under the snow.

Captain Charlie asked Zach and a Gunnison rescuer to help him with the body recovery.

"There is no hurry now. We're dealing with a piece of meat. No chances are to be taken with a life," was Captain Charlie's graphic evaluation. He turned to me and ordered, "I want two carabiners, a hundred and fifty feet of rope, warm gloves and a heavy jacket." He planned to descend from the chopper by rope and tie the rope around the body for the seven-mile dangle to Dunton. But a Huey can't hover long when flying at its ceiling. Instead, the pilots landed below on a flat spot and kept the rotor spinning while the three men climbed 200 feet to reach the body and bring it down. Our C-130 flight was delayed so a team could move in fast should a crash occur during body recovery.

We watched the Huey drift slowly over the spruce, its *whap, whap* filling the Dolores Valley. The aircraft dipped and landed on the hot pool meadow – pre-

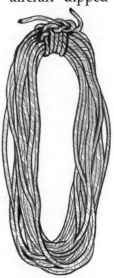

viously the scene of wild joy and unthinkable behavior, now a stage setting for sober rescuers and their visible sorrow. The yet unfrozen body wearing its orange jacket vest was gently lifted out, viewed by the coroner for autopsy information, and zippered into a body bag.

Illuminating moments come from climbing alone – a oneness with the earth – but a modest accident can escalate to grave results.

More grief surfaced when the coroner's report was released. Bill's broken leg and collarbone kept him on the mountain, so he crawled under a rock overhang for protection. He was alone, unseen and

coil of rope

unheard, to hold a three-day vigil with death until the cold and snow of Tuesday's storm brought it to an end.

Our hiker is gone from El Diente, the lodge – bulldozed two years later – is back to the earth from which it rose, the hot pools are filled in with dirt, the searchers are scattered across Colorado. Only the enduring mountain remains – to us the vision of a majestic peak, to the family a nightmare from a solo journey.

13. PROPS

A mission moves with the help of the search dog,
the TV helicopter, the Flight for Life, the flight
nurse and the spouse.

We team members carry the climbing gear, the litter, the ropes and feel the desire and energy to
search up to 13,000 or 14,000 feet. Still, rescue missions come along where that just isn't enough.
Then we turn to an outside strength – a strength that is
always "standing by." This valuable resource comes in
various shapes, sizes and species.

I had slumped over and fallen asleep on the ground, to be
awakened by a pack of dogs. The animals, of great size and
energy, dashed by me, playing tug-of-war and fetching sticks
thrown by their handlers. The dogs were silent – no barking.
Their eyes pierced mine and sparkled with intelligence. I
watched in awe.

Earlier that afternoon, Vickie, a young and earnest dog
handler, and her handsome search collie, Andy – with six
other handlers and their German shepherds from Rocky
Mountain Rescue Dogs – had been flown by the Air Force
from their homes in Ogden, Utah, to Durango in southwest-

ern Colorado. The Fort Carson Chinook then lifted this team to search base in a primitive hunting camp at 11,400 feet in the San Juan Mountains, nine miles north of Wolf Creek Pass.

For over four days ground searchers had unsuccessfully combed the wooded slopes, grassy tundra and rocky drainages surrounding this hunting camp for Scott, a young Minnesota doctor out bow-hunting for elk.

After a briefing, Dick Epley, diligent leader of the Utah team, boarded the Chinook, which was to drop off a dog and its radio-equipped handler at landings of 150-yard intervals along a west-facing ridge at 12,000 feet. Search leaders felt this west-facing slope was a high-priority area. Dog teams (a dog and its handler) would saturate this two-mile-wide, abruptly pitched mountain-side. They were to move down their assigned corridors (search areas) through tree drifts, across crude ravines and over tufts of grass until they reached Beaver Meadow at 10,000 feet in the

leafy valley below. Across the meadow, Beaver Creek twisted its way below a jumbled wall of rock and forest. This flowing creek and its menacing wall were considered a search boundary – an imaginary line that Scott presumably wouldn't cross.

The dogs had sniffed a scent article – clothing worn by Scott and found in his tent. Upon starting down, Vickie's dog alerted, his head lifted and nostrils flaring in the breeze. Andy was air scenting. The slight breeze pushed a scent from below, uphill over the cool, moist stream bed and between ravine walls. Moving more slowly through the thick tree growth and over the fallen timber, Vickie soon lost sight of her off-lead dog. But soon Andy returned, as he was trained to do, to lead lower in the valley, to a shallow flow of water running between two streams. There the dog halted. Vickie looked around – then abruptly realized she had almost tripped on a man's body at her feet. Obscured by a tangle of foliage and wearing camouflage, the bow-hunter was invisible, face down in the water.

Clues, found by hopeful ground teams in previous days (but proven false when the search was over), had indicated that Scott was alive but lost. This startling discovery of the body, for which Vickie wasn't prepared, left her stunned – but not speechless. Her voice, carrying the words of Andy's tragic find, fell like a rockfall upon the ears of the family and rescuers in camp.

Dick broke into Vickie's deluge of words to ask if she had rewarded Andy. She had. I wondered about the reward, and learned that praise and love and play are all that's needed by a search dog.

"Had the dogs not been given a scent," Dick told me, "they would have been looking for any human scent and probably would have found other ground searchers. Sometimes on an alert some distance out, the dog's reaction tells us the person is alive. When the dog gets close and recognizes the scent isn't from a live person, they aren't as excited, but they make the find anyway, for the game playing and for praise from the handler."

This find by a young "air-scenting" collie – his first in the field on a mission – astonished me. I know that human searchers on foot would have found the body only by chance. A slight chance, at that.

The find was made by more than good fortune. Besides highly trained animals and experienced handlers, the mystery of body sweat and of body scent has been explored over recent years. When emitted by sweat glands, your sweat has no odor; only when bacteria enter the scene does sweat produce an odor, or vapor. And these vapors arise from a skin that is like no other skin in the world – your skin grafts accept only your own skin.

William G. Syrotuck, in his fascinating book, *Scent and the Scenting Dog*, explains that man walks or sits in a cloud of his own debris, called "rafts," that continually shed from the outer skin layer and are launched into the constant warm body currents that rise rapidly (125 feet per minute) alongside our body. About a foot and a half above the head, this heat plume disperses out and scatters the debris over the ground. These tiny rafts, each surrounded by a minute vapor cloud, are laden with bacteria, and, combined with body secretions, give off a vapor that is highly characteristic of that person, and that person only. The dog scents on this vapor.

For the dog, there is absolutely no ambiguity about the odor of a scent article. I remember a night search that featured Jessie, the bloodhound. The dog twice attempted to take his handler down over a chaotic pile of jumbo rocks that had crashed from cliffs above and now forbade the midnight passage of a handler. Undoubtedly, the victim had climbed over the rocks during the daylight and left his scent, but the team continued elsewhere, with a frustrated tracking dog.

Syrotuck reminds us that the search dog scents on more than the human body vapor. For example, he scents on damage from a footstep – crushed foliage and disturbed dirt. In lush vegetation and rich loam, the teeming populations of soil bacteria, which feed on the rafts and the breakdown of crushed foliage, produce added and different vapors. Also, when odors of emotion such as fear, or of perfumes or clothing covering the body, or of diet like highly spiced foods, are added to the body vapor, the scent turns complex. And putting a family member of the lost person on a team where a search dog is included is upsetting to the dog. He smells the same bar soap, the same laundry soap and the same food odor which are common to the victim.

Humidity and drizzle enhance conditions for bacteria and, therefore, increase the scent – though a heavy rain washes away this ground scent. Sunlight is bad; ultra violet, violet and blue rays kill the bacteria and reduce the scent. Heat is worse. That is why warm, live bodies in cool air give off more scent than warm, live bodies in hot air. Hot sandy soils or hard surfaces like roads have no moisture or nutrients – indeed, no bacteria.

Dog handlers know these limiting factors, these handicaps to finding a person, and work their dog thoughtfully, always aware of his unique abilities. A German shepherd has 220 million olfactory sensory cells in his nose (man has only 5 million). In the field a dog works that incredible apparatus to scent objects we consider odorless; to scent a subject at night; to scent odors through air-tight containers; to scent a man through a scent pattern; and to scent while he eats, for he can breathe through his nose while swallowing food.

Air scenting isn't the only way dogs are capable of finding a person. A "trailing" dog will work the rafts that are launched along a person's route, sniffing at leaves above ground and moving many yards from the person's footprints. Another searcher, the "tracking" dog, plods from footstep to footstep in head-down position, sniffing the ground like a blood-hound. The traditional tracking dog's nose is 300,000 to 3,000,000 times as sensitive as a man's!

According to Fran Lieser, leader of SARDOC (Search and Rescue Dogs of Colorado), based in Loveland, air scenting is easier to teach and can be taught to a mature dog. Not so for trailing or tracking, where a pup is best.

Trained dogs can be invaluable in avalanche rescue. With little or no air to breathe, a victim's body is packed in ice crys-tals, and his situation is critical. A line of rescuers, probing with long rods to locate the buried person, is slow. Avalanche beacons are accurate and fast only if the buried victim is wearing a beacon on "transmit," and the searcher on the sur-face is holding another beacon on "receive." An avalanche-trained dog, however, is a four-legged, self-contained beacon. With acute sensitivity, his nose pushes hard against the snow and toward a scent – he breathes out side slits in his nostrils. His paws dig deep to aid his sniffing.

In a hard-slab avalanche, formed from snow deposited by wind, the crystals are cold and dry and packed tightly toge-ther. After tumbling during an avalanche, the slabs of snow pile up in chunks to leave air channels which permit rafts and vapors to be carried through the jumbled mass for consid-erable distances by air currents that flow within. An ava-lanche dog will pick up the scent. Hard to believe, but detec-tion through six feet can be expected; in wet snow, detection of two feet is more likely, since snow density and water re-duce passage.

When a person walks through a snow layer, his rafts will lie on the surface. The cold reduces bacterial action, and scent intensity drops; regardless, the dog will track the scent. Per-sons in a snow cave or buried under a snowfall will give off vapors that join with the warm air currents coming from the earth, and together they rise through the snow layer to be detected by a search dog.

If search dogs are invaluable on Colorado rescues then the Denver TV stations' tiny choppers are priceless. Actually a bucket of bolts in a bubble of plexiglass, with a rotor whining overhead, they are often referred to as "Death Rangers" rath-er than the more proper Bell Jet Rangers.

Peter Peelgraine from Denver's Channel 7 showed the inherent courage of TV copter pilots when he and our Ed, a young mission veteran with a thick crop of black hair to top his slender body, were at a September search for a missing hiker. The would-be climber, Tim, wearing jogging shoes and sweats, had moved up onto the severe rock wall of 14,060-foot Mount Bierstadt in the Front Range west of Denver, and tumbled to his death. After a two-day scrutiny of the mountain, Tim's body was found at 13,300 feet.

bubble helicopter

To save the hours and the muscle needed to haul a metal Stokes litter weighing 25 pounds, and 800 feet of rope (four coils of 200 feet), up to the body over a steep scree slope, Ed was asked to load the gear into the little aircraft and then to fly with Peter and drop if off at the site. Ed's expressive face told other members he was scared; still, strong pride in his assignment mingled with the fear. The body was lying in a narrow couloir (a precipitous gorge) filled with loose talus and boulders. As the pilot hovered directly over it – and alarmingly close to the rock wall – Ed hung out the helicopter door and lowered the rescue equipment, carefully spaced along a climbing rope, to the waiting evacuation team. The brave flight of Peter and Ed left no space for errors. Unpredictable winds, swift and swirling, could have sent the bird down. Because of the helicopter assistance, the body recovery was completed just before dark, as an alpine darkness drifted across the sawtooth ridge of Bierstadt.

The TV helicopter and its adventurous pilot have been a godsend to searchers – wings added to boots. Now Flight for Life joins the TV chopper in the air – with space for a victim lying in a litter that fits snugly on the floor beside the pilot. The local Flight for Life rescue helicopter flies out of St. Francis Hospital in Colorado Springs, picking up patients in Colorado and nearby states and delivering them, at a fee, to a hospital of their choice – preferably St. Francis.

Five months after the birth in 1983 of Flight for Life, we worked a shocking mission that convinced me the bird had a warm future in the mountains. Two couples, all in their late teens and riding around at midnight, had gone over an 800-foot sheer drop along Gold Camp Road, west of Colorado Springs. By the time an immature Douglas fir had stopped their tumbling vehicle, all four had been hurled out. Two climbed back up to the road – the other two, a fellow and a girl, lay with fractures on the rocky scree 365 feet below.

Their removal to an ambulance wouldn't be easy; the night was a black hole, and clay earth packed hard as lava covered the precipice above. The rusted wreckage of other auto accidents lay strewn over our path to the lower slopes. I was then in my second summer of rescue, and experience had taught me it was best not to fight gravity; we would go down, not up. A hundred and fifty feet below the victims, a shelf jutted out to one side. I remembered from hiking in the area that the dirt access road to the shelf was long and eroded beyond what an ambulance could handle.

Then I heard the words, "Flight for Life is coming!"

As one of four bringing down the girl's litter, I was too busy to notice the little chopper's approach in the darkness. Like an impetuous bird, it suddenly hovered over the shelf and lowered into a thick growth of wild sweet clover that reached to my waist. Suppose large rocks waited in ambush, or the shelf wasn't level? What boldness, I thought. The rotor wash parted the clover straight down the middle. With knives spinning close overhead, our team slid the litter in the narrow door. We quickly retreated, bent over, with heads tucked into our chest, while the aircraft lifted straight up in the blind night and turned for the hospital. Another team brought the young man's litter from the cliff, just as the chopper returned to part the sweet clover once again.

Such delicate flying maneuvers impress a rescuer; but whenever we rely on a bird, I worry that our team might dilute its strength, its ability to complete a rescue without outside help. Nonetheless, looking back through the mission years, helicopter assists do stand out like gifts from heaven. One night when the sky was black as a cave, five of us responded to a mission involving two fishermen overdue a day in their return from Rampart Reservoir, a fishing paradise in the Rampart Range west of Colorado Springs. Since the men might be in the cold water hanging on to their overturned boat, we raced up at midnight. Just when I suspected a 12-mile trek along the fingered waterline was my fate, Flight for Life volunteered to fly.

With a powerful searchlight protruding between the skids, they traced the shore and sighted a beached fishing boat and a tent. The flight nurse jumped out to knock on the tent flap, and two sleepy fishermen peeked out. To our relief, they had simply decided to remain one more day and hadn't bothered to drive to a phone. I wondered if the flight nurse was trained in the proper way to sound out a tent at midnight. Suppose two brown bears had nosed through the flap? When the Twin Star flew close overhead and radioed its goodbye, I gazed lovingly at the bird that had saved my legs from an all-night stagger.

Ordinarily I'm not happy to see a piece of machinery break the mountain reverie, but now, after almost five years on the team, I've learned what the Flight for Life rotor can do for us. One Fourth of July this diminutive mosquito with bulging eyes cleared a 9,400-foot wooded ridge and dipped straight for us. Her soft whine from the twin turbine engines drifted over our secluded valley on Pikes Peak.

I stood on a pinnacle rock that rose out from the wild grass carpeting the hillside; Tom was next to me talking to the pilot by radio. Below, in a bumpy meadow, seven more rescuers waited by a small tent pitched along a noisy stream. The tent wasn't empty. Inside, Linda, a 40-year-

the Beaver

old Oklahoma woman who had been camping there with her husband for two days, lay on a sleeping bag, her bloated stomach exhausted from cramps and last night's retching, leaving her body dangerously dehydrated.

She listened to the gurgle of the stream that carried the microscopic parasite Giardia in its pristine-appearing water.

Giardia, now in her intestines, come from any vertebrate up-stream – a deer, a coyote or a human – who contaminated the water with his poor hygiene. One can teach a human, but one can hardly potty-train a beaver. Giardia can be knocked from the intestines by Flagyl, an expensive drug, but the affliction must first be diagnosed in a lab. We thought, like her husband, that she had severe flu, for the symptoms are similar.

Linda's weakness in the obscure canyon was a calamity. Her husband had hiked out three miles for our response, but I knew our team's pickings were slim on a holiday. Nine volunteered for the mission – two women and seven men – while two more men stayed below for radio work. Not too shabby considering the big holiday.

Two oxygen tanks, a litter in two pieces, our airplane-tire wheel for removing the litter, rock evacuation equipment, and 600 feet of rope burdened our men. In the heat, I settled for my daypack and an anchor rope. The quaint Manitou Incline lifted the team and gear up to 8,600 feet. From there we hiked over a saddle, down into a low valley and back up to 8,700 feet on the South Fork of French Creek.

The heat and humidity became intense when we started up the South Fork. The trail was the width of a garter snake and about as sinuous. Lush foliage, wet from a mountain storm, hung over the trail and obscured moss-covered roots and slippery earth. If a boot skidded, the member slipped and splashed into the creek many feet below.

"There's no way we're going to get this woman back down this trail in a litter," Mel insisted. "It's either an uphaul to Barr Trail or Flight for Life."

I watched the bird swoop down to case the meadow landing site we had suggested to the pilot. Long streamers of orange flagging fluttered from an aspen and gave wind direction. We believed the small grassy plot was almost level, but Terry Lovell, the pilot, didn't see it that way. He landed on one skid – the other hung daintily in the air – while Linda Sand, a flight nurse, jumped out the door. Then he was up and out of sight.

After the nurse slipped an I.V. into the sick woman's arm vein to replace fluid lost during the night, the aircraft was called back by radio. Four men carried her litter across the sloping meadow, avoiding the tail rotor like they would a scorpion's stinger. Somehow, the helicopter, crammed with

Linda the patient, Linda the nurse, and Terry the pilot, took off into warm, expanded air at 8,700 feet. Nine rescuers and one husband rejoiced.

The men loaded the unused and heavy equipment onto their backs once again and we slid over the trail, across the saddle and down to the Incline – swimming through hot steamy air, some of us drinking quarts of water from the Giardia stream. We laughed and shrugged our shoulders, trusting any acquired resistance to Giardia to get us through.

That Flight for Life out of St. Francis Hospital saved us an incredible amount of time and sweat. Days later I congratulated Terry on his Dance of the Skids. "I was flying into the ground," he explained. "Trying to hold the aircraft on the sod and using as much power as in a hover. And fortunately for you people, I'd just returned from a mission out on the plains and had flown off some fuel." If his tank had been more full, he could have landed – a chopper can always land! – but might have been unable to take off from our elevation on the warm day. Indeed, just lifting off the hospital helipad at 6,000 feet elevation in the summer forces him to hold his fuelweight to 40 percent of capacity.

Terry sobered me further when he added, "If your meadow walls had been steeper, I couldn't have lifted off." A thin line of safety exists for take-off; he had carefully figured in the woman's body weight, refusing her backpack with a wave of his hand.

I've grown to love the single-rotored choppers, smaller and lighter in weight than a Huey; not because they save our back muscles, which they do, but because of their grace and lightness. When in flight, a small helicopter and a tiny hummingbird have much in common, even in their whirling sound effects.

Sometimes the bird can't fly because of the ever-changing mountain weather in Colorado Springs. Maybe he can land on the 14,110-foot summit of Pikes Peak, or perhaps only at the 11,500-foot treeline, or possibly much lower – it all depends on the ceiling. Generally, he figures, "If I can see the Peak, I can fly." In his late 30s, Terry isn't new to choppers. He piloted Huey helicopters and flew geologists around Alaska before Flight for Life. He summed up his philosophy with a positive, crisp remark. "I like to fly and I like helping people. And I really feel my job is worthwhile."

In talking with Linda Sand, chief of the five flight nurses at St. Francis Hospital, I realized that she is one of our breed. The challenge fulfills her – the touch of danger, the rush of adrenaline and the stream of missions that never repeat themselves. Like the rescuer who says to himself after a mission, "Today I did a great thing," she also can say, "Today, I made a difference in that car wreck out on the plains. I was a physician in the field. I was all they had. I was 'it'."

Linda, a gentle woman in her late 20s and with a depth of kindness, was born on a cattle ranch in the high country north of Black Forest, about 40 miles south of Denver, where she lived with the birth and the death of animals. She came to terms with the act of dying, and now accepts the risk of death in a helicopter crash. Working cattle took bravery, just like riding a chopper does now.

Med Pack

But the acceptance of death in her patients is another matter. Despite the emergency care and the aircraft's speed, one-quarter to one-third of her patients die over the next week, because they are so critical when she gets them. In a soft voice, Linda mentions "the sick baby, the car crash or the death of a child – so difficult . . ."

Also, like rescuers, Linda sees the unstable victim. "We fly to a car accident; the arm of an unconscious passenger is hanging out the window. I quickly think, does he need an airway, or an I.V.? Or is it a head injury, or maybe internal bleeding?" She is unaware of the cold and dark night, where only her headlamp lights the way.

I think that stress brings out a person's best. Granted, when riding the helicopter the rise in adrenaline is hard to control; nevertheless, a good nurse, Linda says, must be calm and stable. She must communicate with the rescue worker, the patient, even the rural ambulance medic who has a patient only occasionally and may himself need calming.

I was about to leave Linda so she could continue her 12-hour night shift in the emergency room or in the chopper, when she gave me a pensive, faraway glance. "I'm able to see the beautiful Colorado sunrises, the sunsets, the Sangre de Cristos in winter white, the clouds, the rainbows . . .

The patience of a husband or a wife at home is often forgotten, yet this is a vital ingredient to the team's accomplishments in the field. Since so few women join and most are single, a spouse is usually a woman. The team often rates high in a husband's life – a wife detests the orange shirt as her competition – however, "the other woman" is a mission.

Sleeping spouses, unmoved by adrenaline, are awakened in the depth of night by a pager's piercing tone giving an emergency message in a male voice, and subjected to the noise of frantic dressing and departure. If the spouse wants the car, chauffering is necessary. During the day the tone shatters silence at the sermon, the movie and the restaurant. Dinners turn cold, picnics are canceled, guests are left waiting. Bachelors should contemplate this neglect a spouse suffers.

After a mission, the spouse is forced to listen to endless phone calls from other members, where details are dissected like a frog. Gear is spread across the floor as in a garage sale. Two-hundred-foot nylon ropes are cleaned in the washing machine, and hang for days drying in spaghetti coils from the basement ceiling.

The spouse tolerates these anoyances with a patience worthy of sainthood. Members are aware of these qualities, for we take their spirit with us always.

14. ZEAL

*A rescuer feels compassion, smothers fear with
courage, silences temper and suffers through
embarrassment.*

John, our young victim, sat on a log, basking in the
warm February sunshine that flooded the path to the
historic log cabin at Barr Camp. One bare foot, swollen the size of a skunk and striped black and blue,
stretched in front of him. Unable to stand and greet our team
of seven, he offered, instead, a bashful grin – especially when
he saw our litter and a small aircraft tire.

This rock climber, a senior on spring break from the University of Michigan, had left Barr Camp early the previous
day with a fellow student, to practice on cliffs below the 14,110-
foot summit of Pikes Peak. Ascending a steeply pitched snow
cornice, he lost his balance on the crusted surface. After a fast
skid he crashed into talus rocks, where a boot jammed into a
rock crevice, twisting the bones into fractures. The fall left
him with only one good foot on a snowy summit abandoned
for the winter. Barr Camp was some distance below – two
miles straight down the face and three miles more by bumpy
trail. After sliding across snowfields, crawling over rocks and

creeping along the trail with the help of his friend, an exhausted John reached Barr Camp 10 hours later.

I stood on the trail and stared at the top of John's head – the scalp was split for two inches and the injury appeared recent. "Yeah," he explained. "I lost my balance jumping through the cabin on one foot. Crashed into a door sill." So now we had a man with both ends injured.

After tucking John into a down bag, and tying the bag in the litter that was clamped over the wheel, we ferried him a mile by trail to the cog train tracks. The cog track bed was packed smooth and by laying the wheel against a track – a rope held from behind controlled his speed (a moving brake) – the track steered the litter for a swift two miles to our cars at Ruxton Park reservoir, high on Pikes Peak. A crude and twisted dirt road brought us 11 miles to Gold Camp Road; in another 25 miles of curves we reached the hospital. By then John and his friend were hanging out the door, carsick.

How kind of us to give our day to a stranger. John even wrote, "I don't know what I would have done without your help." But I admit that the excuse to drop our town lives on a Wednesday, to file with friends while talking and laughing and teasing along an aspen-wooded trail buried here and there in snow is what we want most. Each member – Tom, Mike, Kevin, Rudy, Jim Lyon, Jud Smalley and myself – was a comrade-in-arms, not as a soldier but as a friend with a common goal: to shuttle the young student to a plaster cast and some stitches. Sometimes a mission is so enjoyable that I sense my guilt, as though no mission should be pleasurable. "No adventure is good unless you pay the price," I remember reading, the price being miserable conditions. The statement doesn't always fit.

This strong desire to aid strangers stricken by misfortune runs like a vein of gold inside the team. When I joined I had no such sense of mercy – adventure was my goal – but the compassion of the members was contagious and I caught this best of all diseases.

Our mercy reached the ultimate when the young family and old man from Kansas fell into big trouble on Pikes Peak one blizzardy Memorial Day. At dawn, when their rescue was over and we were to load them into the Huey that had touched down on a ridge at 11,500 feet, I overheard an enlightening conversation between two men on our team.

"I'll carry the little girl," Don Hanson, a mountaineer of great warmth, offered.

"No. I'll carry her," Charles Campbell, an architect with a strong personality, corrected him.

"I'll take her," Don repeated.

"Now, look," Charles insisted, "I brought this little girl all the way down the mountain and I will carry her to the helicopter."

Crouched beside the snowsled, Charles lifted her sleeping body from the down bag and hurried across the snowpack. Bending under the spinning blades, he placed her in the waiting Huey. We followed with the sick old man in his litter.

Others knelt to lift the two barefoot boys from the children's sleeping bag onto their tired backs – where the six-year-old urinated over his rescuer's wool shirt on the way to the aircraft. With all four inside, the door was slammed shut. When the rotor blades increased speed for take-off, we hid our faces from rotor wind and stinging ice. And I hid my eyes, filled with tears, from the men beside me – only to discover later that they, too, spilled a few.

I know if money had been involved, a payment for our services, the tenderness that we showed on that mission would have been diminished. Our compassion must have no price.

That we are benevolent is usually obvious, that we are courageous is not, since only the fearful member needs courage. Not all our rescuers see a danger and feel anxious, for their confidence and skill sweep away what, to most of us, would be a frightening risk.

My fearfulness comes and goes. A rappel down a 150-foot vertical cliff on a thin nylon rope after weeks of no climbing causes me to have trembling hands and a dry mouth. Yet any high-angle practice, if held frequently, is sheer joy. The exposure to height doesn't change, only my lack of assurance.

Imagined fears are the worst. I look back to my third summer of searches and remember when seven-year-old twin girls ran across the plains east of Colorado Springs, not intending to return home. After midnight two teams spread

out in a search. With emergency lights flashing on our rescue
vehicle, Kevin (our youngest member but experienced and
eager) and I drove to dark and lonely ranches to obtain permission to search barns.

"Kevin, you drive," I offered. "I'll awaken the ranchers."

"Really?"

"Sure. The voice of an old lady is non-threatening."

To shout the request through a forbidding door to a rancher
– holding a shotgun, no doubt – and to wonder when his
hound would sneak behind my thigh, was a chilling experience. My courage lasted until first light over the prairie,
which chased away the spookiness of the night. The un-
harmed girls were noticed in a vacant house by a paper deliverer, and police returned them to frantic parents. Unknown
to Kevin, I had spent the night pumping up my bravery. That
I could do so was no small matter to me. By this time, of
course, I knew that all wasn't gaiety on missions, for fear
waits beside the trail, above the cliff and inside the Chinook.

Sometimes a member sees a hazard, the chance of death,
and won't accept the exposure. After all, we are volunteers.
"Why should I risk my life for a dead body?" was the reply of
a young rock-climbing member on the team, when asked to
aid in the removal of a climber's body that lay snagged just
below 14,000 feet on the vertical rock of the Crestone Needle
in the Sangre de Cristo Range. Somebody had to bring the
corpse down off the big wall; its presence couldn't be ignored.
Skee, one of our best climbers, was angry with this man's attitude. I understand the refusal – and also the wrath.

How heavy a risk is a rescuer obligated to take in bringing
down the body of a dead stranger? As members of the team,
we are expected to take reasonable risks, but maybe one's family, a spouse and child, take priority over the body of an inexperienced stranger – a man who never should have been
climbing on Crestone Needle in the first place. Many questions exist, with few answers given.

At this time in my life I relish every moment, occasionally
even challenging death through sheer elation; however, I
never laugh at its presence. Moments of great exhilaration occur on rock cliffs where the rope is a lifeline, or in pressing
my face against a Chinook window while it slowly sniffs up a
steep gully packed with windblown snow, reaches the crest at
14,000 feet and glides down the other side, leaving my stom-

ach shrunken and misplaced. And moments of great self-confidence arise from tackling an effort that I think is beyond my ability now that I'm older, and successfully pulling it off.

Unfortunately, with age the self-reliance of youth fades away, to be replaced by a boring conservatism. The ability remains, only the faith in oneself diminishes.

I faced this problem during my first spring on the team. I was hustling along Barr Trail on Pikes Peak with Dave, a long-legged Air Force colonel undaunted by the mountains. Our backs were loaded with a litter and a 200-foot rope for some hypothermic hikers about a half-mile by trail below the summit. With no warning, Dave stepped off the trail and, without an ice axe or uncoiling the rope, started down a steep snow patch alongside a waterfall covered by ice and dribbling water.

"Are you crazy?" I gasped.

"Come on. A shortcut. It'll save time."

With some terror I wedged my feet in his footsteps and started down, feeling melting ice under my boots. When the grade lessened, we plopped in the heavy snow and, in a sitting glissade, flew down the mountainside to a trail switchback below. The shortcut gave me no trouble – only my timidity did.

This caution that grows like fungus in one's later years also strikes young people when they are faced with some violent upheaval in their emotions. Take the case of a strong rock climber in another rescue group who was so blown away by the climbing rescues in Eldorado Canyon behind Boulder, Colorado, that finally he couldn't even lead up a 5.4 rock, which is not a high angle at all. He had assisted at so many serious falls on the massive cliffs that his knowledge of what can happen became overwhelming.

Jim Lyon, a smiling and enthusiastic Army sergeant in our group, presses the same panic button the minute he sees too much air below his boots. When he was an 18-year-old on parachute training, the shroud lines of his main chute tangled and the reserve opened only 200 feet above the ground. With almost every bone from head to foot broken, he was left with an understandable fear of heights. Only with control can he cap the nausea and butterflies and sweating hands that appear when rescue work puts him high.

Jim's stress from heights is invisible. Therefore he doesn't receive support from other members. Jim has been my friend for two years, yet I never knew of the emotional strain, or even the accident, until recently. I wonder what tension other members have that isn't mentioned.

One might say that some stress results from every mission, but members usually say little about it; we just accept what happens. No doubt that is wrong. Some time ago a mission came along that caused severe problems for me and Sue Clifton, a mature woman in her 20s. Both of us had been members over four years, although Sue had been on fewer missions because her TV artwork holds her at the station.

The mission was called on a warm but gusty March evening. Members were to report to Cave of the Winds, a deep limestone cavern in Ute Pass west of Colorado Springs which has been developed as a tourist attraction. The cave lies buried behind yellow cliffs that rise vertically out of slopes covered with piñon pine, yucca and scrub oak. We knew only that a man attending a party had fallen 80 feet from a wall, and we were to bring his body down from the dry wash in which he lay. Even when a deputy said, "He's pretty badly messed up," I casually replied that the team was used to it.

helmet with moveable light

batteries

We started up the crumbling limestone with rescue gear, following Dick, our member and a deputy coroner, who would declare the young man dead. The wash was eroded by downpours into a precipitous gully of loose boulders and giant clumsy steps. Climbing carefully in the black night, headlamps attached to our helmets, we reached the accident site and lifted our heads to look about.

My beam fell upon the top of a man's head – split wide open. The skull was partially empty and the remaining tissue shone vivid pink in my powerful beam. I recoiled in shock and horror. The deputy's warning hadn't prepared me. Other members dropped him on a body bag and I helped zipper him out of sight. I was on the litter-carry to bring him to the dirt road far below; I kept my mind firmly focused on the harsh route down.

That night the memory shattered my sleep – over and over in full color. Even in the dark room with my eyes wide open,

I saw the vision of his head. For many nights I fought a battle to blot out the sight.

Later, at a training meeting, the mission was critiqued. Sue, sitting beside me, exploded with whispers in my ear. "Peggy, you had a husband to come home to. I had no one. And I've never seen a dead man before. It was so bad that for comfort I finally went over and got a relative's dog."

We are taught not to deny or misinterpret a stressful scene. Instead, we should use shock to increase our acceptance of death, to cope inwardly and realize the ugliness of accidents.

To feel stress in rescue work isn't new to members. One might say every emotion is visible or lying in wait under the skin. I didn't realize I had a strong temper until the team opened its ranks to let me in. Then one cold day at Rabbit Ears Pass, my friend Daniel, a computer technician, slipped off his leash. Without thinking, he stepped over me, the mission leader in the field, and began to bark orders. My authority was being challenged; a deep surge of anger burned in my chest. Somehow I kept quiet in front of the other members, determined to settle the matter later in private. After a week my flames were banked, and I went over the incident with him. "If I take the responsibility, I'll give the orders," I told him. To my happiness the score was evened, for less than a year later, Daniel was embarrassed when he forgot his compass on a major search where he was a team leader. I graciously lent him mine.

Outbursts of temper aren't always pleasant, but at least the emotion is out in front, and perhaps the thorn causing the display can be plucked out, preferably out of earshot of others. In my beginning days, if I made a mistake the members were charitable and didn't correct me. Only when Raven, an Air Force officer who bellowed like a bull, lost his temper over one of my errors and yelled at me, did I begin to shape up.

When a mistake is made on practices or missions where lives might be jeopardized, an invisible monster, shame, sinks to the bottom of that member's swamp – until the night. Then it emerges to torment the person lying in the darkness who cannot see beyond his closed eyelids. My mistakes haunt me for three nights, then I distill the lesson and try to put the incident behind me.

Daniel has said kindly to me, "Peggy, your trouble is you get too excited on a mission. So you end up making a mistake. Calm down."

The errors that caused me embarrassment in my early years as a member were lapses in thinking. One Fourth of July afternoon in my second summer on the team I was asked by Skee to set up one of three brake systems, using a sturdy Douglas fir for an anchor. Our mission was to bring down a fractured ankle over dry waterfalls and scree slopes in a tight canyon. To my horror, when my brake rope knot was checked by another member, as is always done for safety, the knot was found to be incorrect. A double sheetbend knot must be perfect, no variations exist. Five people would hang from my knot. I wanted to perish. At home that evening I made 40 double sheetbends.

People who have lived many years don't suffer embarrassments; they've gotten the hang of life. Now in rescue work I've begun all over again, like a dumb kid, in a field in which I desperately want to succeed. No other volunteer effort has the raw challenge, the hard physical demands and the stroking of one's innermost self. No doubt that is why I feel my errors so deeply.

Even Daniel, barely 30 years old, told me, " When I make a mistake, it eats me up inside." Shame will continue to exist, since there's always a rescuer better than you are – or worse than you are. Just as rescuers on the team are more courageous than you are – or more fearful.

My embarrassment started early, the day after I turned in my application to be a probationary on the team. At a mountaineering store, a young salesman repeated my request, "You want to buy a figure eight for rappelling down cliffs?"

"Yes."

He kept staring at me. When out of earshot of other customers, I confided in him: "I've joined Search and Rescue. I also need a swami belt and leg loops, webbing and carabiners." Skepticism. I continued: "I climbed a lot in the early Fifties on the rock cliffs of California's Stoney Point. In the Sierra, too." He

figure eight

seemed relieved. Perhaps he was nervous selling me the potentially dangerous gear. My sons should have bought it for me.

Despite soon becoming a regular member, I felt my position was precarious. I listened carefully, without daydreaming. I tried to get rock-rescue details into my head. I practiced my knots in the dark. By talking less and hiding grouchiness, I tried to blend in. And for high-elevation hiking, I kept my legs and lungs finely tuned; old horses are put out to pasture.

Some years ago a level-system, determining who was qualified for what level of ability, was written by a committee in our group. But, perhaps because we are too busy with vehicles, equipment, trainings, rescue lectures and paperwork in our limited volunteer time, that system has never been implemented. That's good. People prefer to think they are on a higher level than the committee knows they are. Feelings are hurt, and for no good reason. When a mission comes along, the mission leader in the field works with whatever warm bodies volunteer.

That such a philosophy might be true became evident one August afternoon when a Vietnamese woman attempted suicide by jumping 400 feet down a menacing dirt cliff that drops below the Gold Camp Road on its twining way through North Cheyenne Canyon, west of town. Only six people could, and did, respond: Tom, Kevin, Don and his wife Lori (a mostly inactive couple), my son home from college and I, with all variations in experience.

We were barely enough to do the rescue. Four would be on the litter to carry her 1,500 feet farther down the mountainside. Treewraps, where the rope doubles around a sturdy tree and is released gradually by a brakeman and a rope handler, would control our descent in the wild and overgrown canyon. Using a 200-foot rope, nine wraps were necessary to reach the road on the canyon floor where the Flight for Life helicopter had landed. The woman survived her jump, but six people made a skimpy team. It would have been ludicrous for Tom, our leader, to qualify each of us for the rescue. He was happy for any member who appeared on the scene.

I prefer to qualify myself privately. Unfortunately, it took a year before I began to do missions where my efforts didn't surface with errors. The first performance that satisfied me was at an all-night rescue of two teenagers who, with two others, had lost control of their vehicle at midnight and driven over an 800-foot embankment below the Gold Camp Road. I took the scree pack, heavy with about 40 pounds of technical climbing gear, and my own daypack, down to the victim site and never toppled over on the steep and darkened slope. On the litter-carry my feet stumbled between loose, sharp rocks and the carcasses of rusted cars, but I held steady. A triumphant night for me – a near-tragic night for two young people.

In reflecting back over five years in Search and Rescue, I feel that the night search for Grig, a young man lost among the perilous cliffs of Stanley Canyon that rise west of the Air Force Academy, was my high moment. It was in the spring of my fourth year. At midnight, 29 preppies from the Air Force Prep School who were aiding the search, were told to return to the Academy. I would lead them down, but our trail included the hazardous crossing of a slanting and frozen waterfall. For the first time I stood alone and gave orders to myself. After crossing over to test the danger, I radioed that a climbing rope for a safety line must be sent up. When the rope arrived and was rigged, I guided the young men, one by one, over the ice. The resonant feeling of their grateful pats on my back will never be equaled.

One must realize that the devotion I muster for the team, regardless of hour or exhaustion, is also found in other active members. A few are far more zealous than I am. Mike, our radio expert, expressed our attitude well: "My life would be nothing without Search and Rescue."

All of our members need a high level of excitement in their lives – certainly I do. This spark kindles early in the womb, and is fanned into a flame that burns until the final day. The hours spent digging in my flower garden, hiking, peddling my bicycle through the early morning, and working with my husband on our seven rental houses, makes up my

life now that the four children are away. But the searches and
rescues add an uncertainty, a sudden change in plans, a dare
that shakes up my secure and settled way of life. Possibly
members are addicted to the adrenaline that floods our bodies
when we're charging to a mission – or to the drama, the exposure, to unprocessed life. Often that adrenaline sees an
exhausted rescuer through a difficult mission.

Personally, I enjoy a swift derailment in plans and am
charged by an unexpected emergency. When the call came
one Saturday morning in my fifth year for four members to
assist the Chinook crew in their flight to Independence Pass
for possible survivors in a crashed aircraft, our team was
quietly listening to a lecture on cave rescue. Three men and I
were chosen (we had our gear with us!). In 35 minutes we
were 12 miles away – by red light and siren – and airborne for
a dramatic six hours.

People who know our members after working closely with
us on a mission, can understand our drives too well. When
an Illinois hiker, Andy, was lost two nights on Pikes Peak in
midwinter, he said to Chuck Wilt, one of the young and
bearded caretakers at Barr Camp, where he was taken by a
search party, "I'm so ashamed to have caused all this
trouble."

"Don't think anything of it," was Chuck's shrewd reply.
"They live for a mission."

During lulls in a rescue, our team is so filled with energy
and uninhibited in its playfulness that spectators stand and
stare. They seem to wonder what cranks us up. On the recent
mission to Linda, sick with Giardia on the East Fork of French
Creek on the slopes of Pikes Peak, the husband stood rooted
like a tree trunk and never spoke. His eyes darted from Tom
on the radio with the chopper pilot, to those scouting the
landing zone, to men assembling equipment and to two
women tending his wife. Our nine helmets and shirts, all
bright orange, combined with hiking shorts and boots, must
have made quite a sight in the sharp sunlight. If the husband
had heard the appalling puns and good-natured banter – not
to mention the bickering over the route – during our hike
into the valley, his suspicions of our team would have been
confirmed.

In comparison to me, the team is youthful, and I revel in
their enthusiastic approach to problems, their breeziness and

good nature, and their sense of the ridiculous. When I wandered through my middle years, I felt stagnation in my struggle toward personal maturity. The children, the oatmeal, the laundry and the dusting were too easy. In my late years, I see the challenge in Search and Rescue and have become, in Annie's words, a "raving maniac." Nevertheless, I've seen my progress over the five years. Being on the team is hard to describe, but the experience, in all its fullness, is greater than my words could ever express.

Afterword

Tonight, a technical rock team was assembled to fetch from a thousand-foot cliff the body of Michael, a climber who slipped off the ridge between 14,042-foot Blanca Peak and 14,345-foot Ellingwood Point in the Sangre de Cristo Range. When my name wasn't included on the team, I was crushed. After too many minutes, my mind cleared and I faced up to the importance of participating, even though time passes and abilities change. The writing of this book, a 16-month journey into my heart and mind, has only shown me that a person never really changes within.

Index